A CHRISTMAS STORY

A CHRISTMAS Story

BEHIND THE SCENES OF A HOLIDAY CLASSIC

CASEEN GAINES

ECW PRESS

Published by ECW Press
2120 Queen Street East, Suite 200,
Toronto, Ontario, Canada M4E 1E2
416-694-3348 / info@ecwpress.com

LIBRARY AND ARCHIVES CANADA CATALOGUING IN PUBLICATION

Gaines, Caseen, 1986-, author
A Christmas story: behind the scenes of a holiday classic
/ Caseen Gaines ; illustrated by Ian Petrella.

ISBN 978-1-77041-140-1 (bound)
Also issued as: 978-1-77090-414-9 (PDF)
978-1-77090-415-6 (ePUB)

1. Christmas story (Motion picture).
2. Christmas story (Motion picture)—Influence.
I. Title. II. Title: Christmas story (Motion picture)

PN1997.C57G35 2013   791.43'634   C2013-902480-8

Cover design: Jessica Sullivan
Cover images: Center: MGM/UA Entertainment / Photofest; Top to
Bottom: Anne Dean, Ian Petrella, David Monseur, Ian Petrella, Anne
Dean, Ian Petrella, Anne Dean, Ian Petrella
Interior layout: Natalie Olsen, Kisscut Design
Illustrations: Ian Petrella
Index: Terecille Basa-Ong
Printing: Friesens 5 4 3 2 1
PRINTED AND BOUND IN CANADA

For my grandparents,
because it's impossible to think of Christmas
without thinking about you

Table of Contents

My guess is that either nobody will go to see it or millions of people will go to see it because it will catch on. It's the kind of movie that everyone can identify with.

— **Roger Ebert** —
1983

My Christmas Story

by WIL WHEATON

In 1983, all I wanted for Christmas was a slot car track called U.S. 1 Fire Alert! Electric Trucking. It had roads that snaked around buildings, trucks you could load and unload, and this fire truck that had flashing lights and a real fire bell. Whenever my parents took me to the mall, I waited in line as patiently as an eleven-year-old could for Santa (who I knew wasn't the real Santa, but was actually one of his helpers) so I could make sure the big man knew exactly what I wanted. I wrote letters weekly, leaving nothing to chance.

On Christmas morning, my brother, sister, and I woke up with the dawn, jumped on our parents' bed until they woke up, assembled in our hallway, and held hands. Our father walked out into the living room and announced, "It looks like Santa came last night!" We held hands a little tighter, and tried our best to be still. Our mother assured herself that our eyes were closed, opened the hallway door, and led us into the living room.

When my mother gave the signal, I opened my eyes, and there it was: U.S. 1 Fire Alert! Electric Trucking. I squealed with joy, jumped as high as I could, and ran across the room, power sliding in my footie pajamas like a baseball player trying to make a suicide squeeze play. It was already assembled and ready to go. I grabbed a controller and began driving my trucks around while my siblings opened their gifts and our parents beamed.

I can remember that moment today, thirty years later, as clearly as if I were in the living room in that house right now. I can hear Bing Crosby singing "White Christmas" on the radio, and I can feel the rough gold shag carpeting beneath me as I drove my trucks and the fire engine — with its ringing bell and flashing red lights — around and around.

Coincidentally, *A Christmas Story* was also released in 1983. I didn't know that it would become a classic film, but I knew that it was going to be a great film, because I had auditioned for the part of Ralphie the year before. I was just ten years old at the time, but it made me laugh in all the right places, and it told a story that I could relate to in more ways than I could articulate. I auditioned a lot back then, and I hardly ever read entire scripts, but once I started reading *A Christmas Story*, I couldn't put it down. I didn't book the job (can you imagine anyone other than Peter Billingsley as Ralphie?), but just as I can recall with photographic clarity that Christmas morning in 1983, I can also recall the callback I had for the movie.

The auditions were held on a cold, rainy day in spring, at a casting office in Venice, California. I saw the same kids that I always saw on auditions: Sean Astin, Keith Coogan, this kid named "Scooter" who had a weird mom, and Peter Billingsley, who was very well known at the time, because he was Messy Marvin in commercials for Hershey's chocolate syrup. I sort of knew Peter, because we'd been on so many auditions together, but I was always a little starstruck when I saw him. That day, we talked about *Tron* and *The Dark Crystal*, and the video games we were playing at the time. We were too young to feel competitive, and I was just happy to know so many of the kids in this cold, damp waiting room with even colder metal folding chairs, concrete floors, and bright blue walls.

The scenes we read were the one where Ralphie is telling Santa what he wants and panics, the one where Ralphie is decoding the *Little Orphan Annie* message, and the one where he thinks he shot his eye out. I remember how I felt like I was getting away with murder by saying "son of a bitch" in front of a whole room of adults.

I remember that my dad took me on the audition, and helped me learn my lines. I can still see my dad, in all his permed, mustached, corduroy-pantsed 1982 glory, helping me understand how badly Ralphie wanted that BB gun, not knowing that one year later I would know exactly how Ralphie's BB gun mania felt, when I experienced my own slot car mania. It's a really happy memory, because my dad and I didn't do too many things together when I was a kid, and I always loved it when he'd take me on an audition.

From VHS to DVD, long before it joined *The Twilight Zone* as a must-watch television marathon event, *A Christmas Story* became *The* Christmas Story. And it's easy to see why. Jean Shepherd's narration and dialog is as timeless as his characters are relatable. How many of our fathers also worked in profanity the way other artists worked in oils or clay? Peter just *is* Ralphie. That sweet, guileless kid who you can't help but like? That's who he was in all the waiting rooms in all the auditions I ever saw him in when we were kids. That fast-talking wiseass whose mouth writes checks his body can't cash? Scotty Schwartz is *still* that guy; it's no wonder he was the perfect Flick. And it's no wonder that *A Christmas Story* is not just *The* Christmas story for me. It's *The* Christmas story for a generation.

In fact, maybe it's better to call it *Our* Christmas Story, because it's a gift from Bob Clark and Jean Shepherd that we get to open up year after year after year, and it never disappoints.

Merry Christmas. I hope it's a good one.

And don't shoot your eye out.

Wil Wheaton is an actor (*The Big Bang Theory, Stand By Me, Eureka, The Guild*), writer (*Just a Geek, The Happiest Days of Our Lives, Memories of the Future*), and producer (*Tabletop*). He lives in Los Angeles, blogs at wilwheaton.net, and is on Twitter @wilw.

Christmas Revisited:
Minor Disasters and Happy Endings

by EUGENE B. BERGMANN

A *Christmas Story* is not only the funniest, but the most witty, most clever, and most satisfying film you're ever likely to see for twenty-four hours straight starting Christmas Eve.

Over 50 million people watch at least parts of it every year as it's shown on cable television, and some families, in their Christmas passion, have memorized the dialogue and the narration, repeating them along with the film. Yet most of the viewers undoubtedly don't know much about the background of the film. If their ignorance is bliss, this book will improve their bliss by filling in a lot of background — and foreground.

Focus for a moment on the creator of this masterpiece. Let's begin *A Christmas Story* with its opening titles. Of course not enough people read film titles, but in this case it's worth taking the trouble, because who created it and narrates it are of much relevance to what it's all about. The vast majority of the film's annual viewers probably don't know who Jean Shepherd is, despite the fact that prominent among the opening titles they could read Shepherd's name four times: that this was a film "from the works of Jean Shepherd"; that Ralphie's adult voice was none other than Shepherd; that the movie was based on Shepherd's story collection, *In God We Trust, All Others Pay Cash*; and that Shepherd cowrote the film script with his wife, Leigh Brown, along with the film's director and co-producer, Bob Clark.

Jean Shepherd, for all the humor and joy he expressed in his decades of nightly radio programs, also had a negative view of life — he called it "realistic" — and he definitely disliked nostalgia, even though it sometimes crept into his work, especially at the tail-end of a film such as *A Christmas Story*. Although Bob Clark once said that they worked hard to give a recognizable sense of what many people would remember from their past, he did not suggest that the film was meant to be an exercise in nostalgia. Clark called it "an odd combination of reality and spoof and satire." That is not nostalgia.

As to negativity and nostalgia, one has only to think about most of the film's calamitous set pieces. Yet, because they are so funny, most people don't realize that the funniness is inseparable from the bizarre outcome of so many incidents:

- Flick's time at recess ends with his tongue getting painfully stuck to a metal pole.

- On the crate containing the Old Man's major award leg lamp, a stenciled sign, poorly positioned on the lid, serves as a critique of the Old Man: missing the beginning letter T, it says, "HIS END UP." Later, the symbol of the Old Man's triumph is reduced to nothing but a pile of broken glass and plastic.

- When Ralphie says the "F" word while helping out his father, he blames his innocent friend Schwartz for teaching him the word (causing Schwartz's undeserved pain and anguish), and, as punishment, Ralphie has a bar of Lifebuoy soap stuck in his mouth. Convinced he'll go blind, he'll at least enjoy making his parents feel guilty.

- Ralphie's boundless joy at finally receiving his *Little Orphan Annie* decoder pin is deflated by "a crummy commercial."

- Nasty Santa's big black boot, descending toward Ralphie's face, gives him a no-more-nonsense-out-of-you tap on his forehead, propelling him down the slide — not your usual image of jolly Ol' St. Nick.

- Back home, when the lights go out as the father decorates the tree, narrator Shepherd comments: "The Old Man could replace fuses quicker than a jackrabbit on a date." One need only remember what rabbits are famous for and imagine what jackrabbits would be doing on a date.

- The Bumpus hounds steal the Old Man's greatly anticipated Christmas turkey. Shepherd, the narrator, prefaces the scene by giving us his humorous and ironic view of life in general: "Ah, life is like that. Sometimes at the height of our revelries, when our joy is at its zenith, when all is most right with the world, the most unthinkable disasters descend upon us." It's a funny line to precede what happens, but think about Shepherd's statement seriously for a moment.

- On Christmas morning, surrounded by gifts under the tree, Ralphie's kid brother, Randy, is overcome with the holiday spirit: "That's mine! That's mine! Oh boy, that's mine!" As the narration puts it, both kids quiver with "unbridled avarice," not the best way to celebrate the birth of Jesus. Regarding the pink bunny-pajama gift, our narrator gets to pull a little insider's joke, commenting, "Aunt Clara had for years labored under the delusion that I was not only perpetually four years old, but also a girl." (Shepherd's best buddy, kids' poet and cartoonist Shel Silverstein, wrote Johnny Cash's "A Boy Named Sue" as a friendly poke in the ribs at Jean and his "girl's name" — not the first time they'd kidded each other in public.) With unconscious sexual innuendo, Mom drops in Dad's lap a wrapped bowling ball. He responds with a high-pitched castrati's "Thanks a lot!"

- "Did you get everything you wanted?" the Old Man asks Ralphie, who says, "Oh, almost." The dad responds with a bit of Shepherd-like truth: "Almost, huh? Well, that's life." But the Old Man has bought Ralphie a Red Ryder BB gun to make his life — at least for the moment — seemingly perfect. Ralphie, with loaded gun in hand, is the personification of "armed and dangerous." He sets up a target in the backyard, and gets ready to shoot. The scheming kid has gotten his wish.

And here comes a comment on our family entertainment. How many viewers notice that the support for the target is an advertising sign, maybe from some commercial emporium that had discarded it as useless? One has to look fast for a clue to the film's ironic comment about nostalgia — that upended, sideways sign, in beautiful, old-fashioned, pure white script, in a fleeting reminder of the good old days, announces the soda's brand simply: "Golden Age." That discarded sign, of some resilient metal, propels the ultimate comeback to Ralphie's first shot, ricocheting that BB at him so fast it almost shoots his eye out. Some day the kid might learn the worldly, savvy, adult adage "Be careful what you wish for." Perhaps this is why Shepherd originally wanted to title the film *Santa's Revenge*.

Although Jean Shepherd's philosophy tended to be that most things in life were going to end in disaster, in *A Christmas Story* he was able to present this in an acceptable form, disguising a negative undercurrent and making people laugh with his ever-present humor. After all, much laughter in life springs from a bit of ironic recognition of hard truths unexpectedly made manifest.

Besides, the unpleasant stuff really isn't so bad — in fact it's mostly sort of unreal. For example, Scut Farkus is an overexaggerated caricature of a generic schoolyard bully, and he gets his comeuppance in the end. Losing the Christmas turkey gives the father the opportunity to save the day and also to bring the family together in the funny (politically incorrect) Chinese restaurant scene. The father, indeed, is somewhat unreal in a cliché, cartoony way, somehow rather simple-minded in his pleasures, obsessions, and disgruntlements, but he comes through in the end with the coveted BB gun — he's got love and a heart as big as all indoors. All resentment between Father and Mother dissolves in the final scene of a picture-postcard, gently falling snow accompanied by Christmas tree lights. Humor, contentment, love. Who could ask for anything more? We love this movie because, in some important way, we believe in it.

My family and I watch bits and pieces of the Christmas classic each year between other holiday activities, maybe once or twice sitting through the whole thing, knowing what comes next, enjoying it and laughing as if seeing it for the first time, right down to the film's final scenes. Ralphie and kid brother each happily in bed with his favorite present, and the parents sharing an affectionate moment, scenes that might well have been mandated by the film studio: nobody wants to see a family movie about Christmas, our happiest season, end under an anti-nostalgic cloud. On our TV screen, left on for most of the day, *A Christmas Story* will start anew in a moment, almost endlessly, during that twenty-four hour orgy of delight, and it will be there next Christmas Eve again when we participate in our pleasurable ritual, our reaffirmation of our happy past and hopes for the future. We, my family along with millions of others, smile contentedly and laugh all over again — all is right with the world. That's entertainment.

No matter what else they accomplished creatively, Shepherd and Clark will forever be celebrated for this joint achievement — and Shepherd was proud of the film. In what may have been his last written piece, for *The Age of Videography* in 1996, without question referring to *A Christmas Story*, he wrote, "I must say big-screen movies beat them all. Sitting in a dark movie house, watching your work on the screen and hearing paying customers laugh is one of life's great experiences."

Many of those familiar with Shepherd's work believe that his stories, including those upon which the film is based, are at least somewhat autobiographical. Not so, he insisted — they are all fictional creations. The "true" elements in most of his works are but minor details demonstrating what life is like, rather than depictions of real events. In his stories, he often used real names from his childhood, but this seems just a way to confuse and conflate fact and fiction for his own pleasure. His radio technique convinced many that all his stories and commentaries actually happened to him. He was undoubtedly the most skilled faker in the business.

To repeat the irony that's symptomatic of Jean Shepherd's career, most people who love the film don't even know who he is. Shepherd's most ardent fans consider his decades of radio work to be his supreme achievement, and they also appreciate *A Christmas Story* as a worthy masterpiece — it not only comments with humor on human experience, but it is sublime, chock-full of life's petty afflictions and heartwarming joys. Thankfully, Caseen Gaines' book, while giving us the lowdown on the making of the film, and all that surrounds it, will also increase knowledge of that insufficiently recognized American genius, Jean Parker Shepherd.

Eugene B. Bergmann's book, *Excelsior, You Fathead!: The Art and Enigma of Jean Shepherd*, is a description and appreciation of Shepherd's creative work. Bergmann's transcriptions of dozens of Shepherd army stories can be found in his *Shep's Army: Bummers, Blisters, and Boondoggles*. And covering all aspects of Shepherd's life and work is Bergmann's blog, http://shepquest.wordpress.com.

Introduction

My Google Maps app sent me down Rowley Avenue, a tiny side street in Cleveland that was the last turn before the main attraction — the house that had been completely gutted and lovingly restored to transport tourists back in time to 1983, when the location was used for the exterior shots of the Bob Clark film *A Christmas Story*. Before I realized my destination was in sight, a man with a bright yellow jacket rose deliberately, but slowly, out of his aluminum lawn chair, which was placed at the end of a large stretch of burnt grass in front of his house. He had angled

© Meredith Poczkalski

himself so he could see the interested parties coming from blocks away. As his neon orange flag started waving aggressively in the air, I recognized that my attention was being sought.

"This place must really be busy," I thought. It was a Friday, around 11 a.m., in late January, so I was a little taken aback that the place could attract so much business off-season that they would need to hire someone to regulate the parking.

He seemed to be shouting something at me, but since my windows were rolled up to avoid the Midwestern temperature, I couldn't make out what he was saying. My slow-moving car and what must have been a confused look on my face caused him to wave the flag more vigorously. Sure enough, my intuition was right. There was a large cardboard sign — "Christmas Story House Parking: $5.00" — tied to his fence that appeared to have been written very carefully with a thick-tipped permanent marker. My lime green sedan, which was probably another indicator that I wasn't from around these parts, joined two other cars parked in the lot.

The man introduced himself to my friend Josh and me. There was some overly friendly small talk, then what seemed to be a carefully-rehearsed-to-sound-completely-casual explication of how we should navigate our tour.

"I always tell people to start at the gift shop," he said, pointing to a building across the street at his ten o'clock. "People always want to go straight to the house, but I always tell people to start at the gift shop." We hadn't disagreed with him, but he must have felt compelled to emphasize the point anyway, just in case we had the same thought process as those who had previously ignored his advice.

"Then you should make your way to the museum while you wait for your tour," he said, pointing across the street to a different building, directly ahead. "There's a whole lot to see in there."

I looked across the street, sizing up these two buildings dedicated solely to memorializing the megahit movie that has only grown in popularity with

each passing year. Two more cars on Rowley made their way in our direction. While Josh and I were getting a tour of the grounds that would have been better enjoyed with a pair of binoculars, our tour mates were bypassing the opportunity to park on the lawn and opting instead for the more economical meter-free parking curbside. I must have seemed like the perfect candidate for the man's flag-waving trick, and after seeing the other tourists get out of their cars without forking over some green, Josh and I began to feel we had overpaid for what should have been free parking.

We were, however, getting our money's worth in free advice. "Then, the actual house is right here." He pointed with his flag to his immediate left, to a home best remembered as the one in which Ralphie Parker lived throughout the late 1930s to early 1940s with his whiny kid brother, Randy, his well-meaning and slightly naive mother, and his gruff father (the Old Man) with the heart of gold that was hidden beneath a tough exterior. The house seemed as though it had been untouched over the last twenty-something years, even down to the Christmas lights hanging off the roof and the leg lamp proudly displaying the glow of electric sex in the front living room window.

Josh paid the man and we proceeded to the gift shop, which was stationed in the first floor of a small house. Upon opening the door, I felt like Dorothy transported from her ho-hum monochromatic Kansas farmhouse into the extravagant Technicolor experience that is Munchkinland. There was so much *everything* in the gift shop. I saw figurines of Ralphie in his pink bunny suit. On a separate wall hung replicas of the signature long knit stocking cap worn by Schwartz, Ralphie's potty-mouthed friend. To my right were T-shirts with phrases like "You'll

The *Christmas Story* House Gift Shop © Caseen Gaines

shoot your eye out!" sprawled across the front, and, to the right of them, on an adjacent wall, an army of leg lamps stood in an assortment of sizes, waiting and ready to march into a plastic bag and a living room window near you.

As we moved deeper into the shop, we realized what we had just seen was only the tip of the iceberg. There was *Clarkworld* on DVD, an independently produced documentary about the film's director Bob Clark, on a spinning rack with the film's 1994 sequel, *My Summer Story*. I turned my head and saw officially licensed *Christmas Story* Monopoly, magnets, postcards, action figures, bobbleheads, nightlights, Christmas tree ornaments, puzzles, mugs, and Lifebuoy soap, the cleaning agent used by Ralphie's mom to wash his mouth out after she finds out her son uses foul language while helping the Old Man change a flat tire.

But of everything in the store, what seemed to be most abundant was cash. There were over a dozen other customers in the small store with us. When we went up to the register to make our purchases, it was impossible not to notice the armfuls of stuff with which other people approached the counter. I have to admit, I accidentally gasped aloud when I heard the cashier tell the person ahead of me in line that their total was over $400, which inadvertently made me feel downright thrifty for spending around fifty bucks.

We made our way out of the gift shop and to the museum. About ten people were heading in for the next scheduled tour, some eating kettle corn made and sold by a guy stationed between the house and the lawn where my car was parked.

I had thought that its name, the *Christmas Story* Museum, would be a misnomer. I'd expected to see some signed autographs, maybe the shooting script, and the movie playing on a constant loop. I couldn't have been more wrong. When you go to the *Christmas Story* Museum, you actually are visiting a museum. I had heard of other galleries dedicated to movies, like the Oz Museum in Wamego, Kansas, but I was genuinely gobsmacked at how much material had been amassed about *A Christmas Story* in this one central location. There were glass cases with original props and costumes, framed movie posters in different languages from all over the world, a large handmade dollhouse in the image of the Parker home, and Jim Moralevitz.

Oh? You don't know who Mr. Moralevitz is? Don't worry, I didn't either.

"Good afternoon, and welcome to the *Christmas Story* Museum! I'm one of the actors in the movie." Boy, this guy was very friendly. In fact, everyone we had met so far had been seemed indisputably friendly, including the man who I still felt had swindled me out of five bucks to park on his dead grass. The Christmas Spirit was alive and well in Cleveland, as was the entrepreneurial spirit.

Jim Moralevitz (center) with fans Michael Miller and Kyle Mueller © Michael Miller

Jim Moralevitz was an older gentleman with an easy charm, a naturally friendly demeanor, and a face as unrecognizable to me as his name. "I'm the guy who delivered the leg lamp in the movie!"

I studied his face as he continued to tell us anecdotes from the shoot and how lucky he was to get screen time, even though he hadn't expected any. I found some of his stories genuinely interesting. For example, the prop department had accidentally made the major award's wooden crate too big and it wouldn't fit through the door, which obviously posed a problem while filming. Instead of waiting for a new prop and incurring shooting delays, Bob Clark ordered the crate to be cut until it fit through the entryway. As a result, in some shots, "FRAGILE" is missing its first letter.

While I listened intently to the man's story, he remained completely unrecognizable to me, even though I had seen the film dozens of times. He had 8x10 glossy screen grabs of him in the film that he volunteered to sign for a nominal fee. I expressed to him that I had appreciated listening to him, which was true, and politely declined purchasing his autograph. He remained cordial, nonplussed even, which made me feel relieved because I certainly hadn't meant to offend. As I went from that room of the museum to the next, I could hear him starting all over again for the next set of *Christmas Story* devotees.

It was almost time for our tour of the house, so we headed back across the street. My car was still there, one of the few on the lawn, and the man was still waving his flag as tourists smarter than us drove past him and lined the curb. Without much effort, we spotted license plates from Indiana, Illinois, New York, and Florida. There were a few folks waiting on the porch when we arrived back at the house, their faces pressed to the front window to get a glimpse inside, much like the kids at the beginning of the movie, outside of Higbee's department store. They took what seemed like dozens of photos of the leg lamp from the outside of the house. Every once in a while someone would shout a line like, "It's a major award!" or "Fra-gee-lay!" as their hand mimicked the Old Man's syllable-emphasizing gesture in the film.

We proceeded inside and our friendly tour guide spoke to us in the foyer beneath the staircase of the house, between the kitchen and living room. She gave us some background history about the house, its owner Brian Jones, and the film. She may have spoken about some other things, but after a minute or two, it was hard to pay attention to her. We were *in* the Parker house! The excessively tinseled Christmas tree was about twenty feet away from where

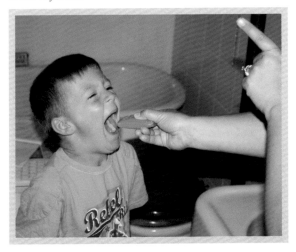

I stood, complete with wrapped gifts underneath as if we were just moments away from Ralphie and Randy waking up in an upstairs bedroom and tripping over each other to get to the presents first. Did a model zeppelin lie underneath, perhaps, or maybe a heavy blue bowling ball that would eventually end up in the Old Man's lap? I found myself craning my neck around the other tourists to see if I could find the long, rectangular gift-wrapped present hiding Ralphie's requested rifle. Everything was almost exactly as I remembered it, but only almost, like when you're up close at a concert and the lead singer looks a little bit different in real life.

After the guide's brief presentation, we were free to roam the house with no stated restrictions. Before we were left to our own devices, we were told that when we got to the bathroom, we were free to put the soap in our mouths. According to our guide, lots of people liked to do that. As we made our way around, Josh and I saw a guy who appeared to be in his early thirties put on Randy's bib and sit at the kitchen table to demonstrate "how the little piggies eat," an homage to the scene when Ralphie's kid brother plants his face in a dinner plate of meatloaf and mashed potatoes. Across from him, a slightly younger-looking woman crawled underneath the kitchen sink and whined, "Daddy's gonna kill Ralphie!" When we got upstairs, we spotted two older women using the phone, pretending to hear Schwartz's mother screaming on the other end upon hearing the news that her son was teaching his classmates dirty words.

Josh and I weren't just people watching, we were playing along too. He put on Flick's aviator hat, which was inexplicably placed on a coat rack near the front door, and I ran under the Christmas tree and took pictures with a Red Ryder BB gun, grinning from ear to ear. When we made our way upstairs, Josh put on the headpiece to the "pink nightmare" pajamas, and I recreated the "Don't forget to drink your Ovaltine" sequence while sitting on the toilet — lid down, of course.

We became kids again, even if just for a few minutes, and everyone around us was a kid too. It reminded me of when I was younger and my friends and I used to play Teenage Mutant Ninja Turtles during recess. There were often several different scenes going on at the same time, and perhaps even more than one kid would be playing Raphael or Leonardo, but we would all be having fun playing some form of the same game.

As we were leaving, I couldn't shake some of the questions that were buzzing around my head. The "how" questions were easiest: how did *A Christmas Story*, a small-budget film that had disappeared from movie theaters by Christmastime of its release year, become one of the most popular holiday movies of all time, surpassing even *It's a Wonderful Life* on some critics' lists? How did this section of Cleveland become a *Christmas Story* mecca, a sort of Disneyland set among the background of steel mills, and how did its owner, Brian Jones, gain the participation of the cast, crew, and Warner Bros. on this unprecedented business venture?

The "why" questions were harder, like why were so many people flocking to this house on a side street in Ohio in the middle of a weekday? I knew what had brought me there — I had just started thinking about writing this book and wanted to check out the house for research — but what about the person ahead of me in line at the gift shop who had dropped a significant amount of cash on merchandise? Why was he there? Why did being in that house turn what I had imagined to be otherwise unexciting adults into giddy children? Why was this middle-America town a major tourist attraction — the Graceland of Christmas? And why was everyone so nice?

Over the next several months, as I spoke to Brian Jones and consequently the majority of the film's cast, members of the crew, friends of Jean Shepherd and Bob Clark, and other *Christmas Story* fans, the answers to many of these questions became clearer. With train conductors Shepherd and Clark, this movie was the little engine that could. The film defied the

Fans Stephenee Carsten
and Cory Kross
© Stephenee Carsten

odds and skepticism of the executives at MGM, the studio that released the picture, to become not only a holiday classic but also one of the most watched broadcasts on television during the week of Christmas, thanks in no small part to the twenty-four-hour marathon airings started by television mogul Ted Turner in 1997. The most popular lines from the film have easily slipped into our pop lexicon, and the most ardent fans of the film can incorporate even the most esoteric pieces of *Christmas Story* dialogue into their everyday speech. (One of my personal favorites is exclaiming "Nottafinga!" whenever I leave a room and want my things undisturbed while I'm gone.) There have been annual conventions dedicated to the film, multiple home video releases on VHS, DVD, and Blu-ray, and public appearances by cast members at events over the last ten years.

When I was interviewing people for my previous book, *Inside Pee-wee's Playhouse*, I found that most people I spoke to were surprised I was calling. They hadn't spoken about the popular children's television show in decades and, especially when I was just getting started, they couldn't figure out why anyone would be interested in writing a book about a 1980s television show. Of course, people were still interested in Pee-wee Herman, but those inside the bubble seemed unaware of it.

Conversely, there wasn't a single person I interviewed for this book who didn't recognize the amazing significance of *A Christmas Story*. This film is more than just an impressive credit on a resumé for the crew; it's Bob Clark and Jean Shepherd's love letter to the world. Unlike those of any other film that I can think of, the cast members of this movie remain in contact with one another — with some notable exceptions — and in strong alliance when it comes to participating in events, attending conventions, and granting interviews. It's all for one and one for all. There are many reasons why this may be, but it's safe to say that this particular relationship among cast members of a movie that's three decades old is unique. Unlike long-running television shows, actors typically work on a movie for only a few months, perhaps a year, tops. It's not that common that lifelong friendships and professional relationships develop as a result of working on a film. However, the *Christmas Story* featured players continue to defy convention every time they appear together at a promotional event — which is actually more often than you might realize.

Whenever I told a friend or co-worker that I was writing a book on *A Christmas Story*, their reactions always took me by surprise. They would go on about either their love for the film or, more frequently, their love for Jean Shepherd. It seemed as though many people's appreciation for the movie was grounded solely in the fact that the film was based on his work. I knew Shepherd was immensely popular, and he has remained so thanks in large part to his published works and a number of extremely comprehensive fan sites on the internet, but I hadn't realized the full reach of his impact.

Ian Petrella signs autographs © David Monseur

For those uninitiated into the Cult of Shepherd, the reaction was equally as passionate. Sometimes the casual mention of this project would produce ten minutes of debate about which scene from the movie was the best. Personally, my favorite moment is when Miss Shields, played by Tedde Moore (one of the nicest women on Earth), is trying to guilt Ralphie and Schwartz into admitting they got Flick to touch the flagpole with his tongue. But many people disagreed with me. How can you go without laughing when the kid brother Randy is bundled up so tight that he looks like "a tick about to pop?" Who isn't reminded of a father figure in their family when the Old Man shouts obscenities at his furnace, or when he fails to mask his dignified heartbreak when his wife breaks his beloved leg lamp? Or what about the Chinese restaurant waiters, who are laugh-out-loud funny even though the joke is far beyond politically correct?

But almost always, this question would come up: "Why are you writing a book about *A Christmas Story*?" When I explained the brief history of the film, and its sequels, stage adaptations, and the *Christmas Story* House in Cleveland, most of the people I spoke to were dumbfounded. "They made a sequel?" I think most people didn't believe me. "There's a museum? *In Cleveland*?"

The irony became crystal clear early on. There is a whole section of the population that has seen this film dozens of times, and many who cite it as their favorite movie of all time, and yet know virtually nothing about it. I found this fascinating, and the more I told people about the movie's journey in becoming one of the most beloved holiday flicks of all time, the more people wanted to hear.

Like a family member, *A Christmas Story* is loved. It's the last thing I see as I fall asleep before Santa Claus comes to visit, and the soundtrack to my Christmas morning while we open gifts. For my family, and for many others, it's a part of our annual holiday routine. For those who worked on the film, the love hasn't faded in the thirty years since the movie was shot. Even those who hadn't spoken about their work in decades enjoyed revisiting the house on Cleveland Street.

As Josh and I made our way back to the car and drove off, I couldn't stop thinking about the untold *Christmas* stories. What was it about the movie that made it stand the test of time, and why was the film such a dominating force in our popular culture three decades after its debut? I didn't know, but after visiting that alarmingly busy side street in Cleveland, I knew I had to find out.

CHAPTER ONE

The Ten-Year Itch

Somewhere in Coral Gables, Florida, a young Miami-based filmmaker named Bob Clark was doing his sixth lap around an unfamiliar neighborhood.

An hour earlier, he was getting into his car, on his way to pick up a date. He was dressed nicely, as a young gentleman should be, and made every effort to be punctual. However, on the way to his date, he became sidetracked.

Derailed.

Pre-occupied.

He fell in love.

As any young man will attest, it is easy to find oneself overcome with romantic feelings for a number of things. Send the sexiest woman in the world in to talk to a man during the Super Bowl and she may find herself waiting until the nearest commercial break to be noticed. Try to interfere with Mr. Fix-It's D.I.Y. project and you may be able to steal a few minutes of conversation, as long as you agree to hold the screws in the interim. If there's a *Star Wars* marathon on and you're not wearing a Princess Leia wig, you can forget about it, especially if you're dating a member of the ComicCon crowd. Young men are simpleminded creatures.

Clark's newfound infatuation was a man's voice on his car radio. That voice belonged to Jean Shepherd. And like your typical young man in love, Clark found it hard to end his first tryst. He prolonged the inevitable conclusion by taking the scenic route to his date's house, while Shep, as fans of his radio show affectionately called him, continued to tell his tale.

Jean Parker Shepherd was born on July 26, 1921, on Chicago's South Side. His family moved soon after to 2907 Cleveland Street in the Hessville section of Hammond, Indiana. Before graduating Hammond High School in 1939, Shepherd, like Bob Clark, also fell in love with radio. He received his Amateur Radio license at age sixteen — although some accounts state that he might have caught the radio bug even earlier than that — which ended up being the first step toward a long career as a great communicator.

Jean Shepherd in 1961
© Photofest

His radio skills were first put to use between 1942 and 1944 when, during WWII, Shepherd served as a part of the United States Army Signal Corps. Four years later, he landed his first job as a radio personality on WSAI out of Cincinnati. Between 1951 and 1953 he worked at radio station KYW in Philadelphia, but soon found himself back in Cincinnati at a different station, WLW.

It has been reported, largely by Shepherd himself, that he was offered the hosting job on NBC's *Tonight Show* by then host Steve Allen, who was preparing to relinquish his duties as master of ceremonies. While in Cincinnati,

Shepherd hosted the late-night show, *Rear Bumper.* The story goes that Allen saw Shepherd's show, was impressed, and wanted him to be his successor. The problem was, NBC executives were contractually bound to offer Jack Paar the gig first. If he declined, as the suits thought he would because they assumed he wanted a show during prime time and was uninterested in a late-night slot, Shepherd would be crowned the new heir to the *Tonight Show* throne. The execs were so certain, in fact, that they flew Shep out to New York to prepare for the job, only to find out soon after that Paar had accepted. The young radio guy's primary contribution to the *Tonight Show* from that point on would be as a member of the viewing audience.

Jean Shepherd in WOR studio in 1970 (Ofindsen)

According to those familiar with Shep's biography, there is little evidence to support that there's much truth to that story. Much like one of the tales told by Estelle Getty's Sophia Petrillo on *The Golden Girls*, Shepherd's story would have placed him just a half-step away from achieving a level of fame in his early thirties that most people can only dream about. However, even if the story is false, *something* brought Shepherd out to New York City in 1955, and that something could be given credit for the next exciting chapter in his life at WOR.

When one searches the internet for information about Shepherd, what comes up most frequently is that he is "an American raconteur." This phrase wouldn't necessarily be unusual, except that the term "raconteur," which is hardly ever used, is almost uniformly regarded as the official term for his job description.

Dictionary.com defines a raconteur as "a person who is skilled in relating stories and anecdotes interestingly." What, then, made Jean Shepherd so recognized as such an *interesting* storyteller?

"What comedians like to do is take something they want to make fun of, that they want the audience to have fun with, and what they will do is talk

Bob Clark © Ian Petrella

about what's wrong with it and why it's stupid," comedian Jerry Seinfeld said in a 2012 appearance honoring Shepherd's career. "[Shepherd] did the exact opposite in so many cases. It's a very difficult trajectory in comedy to say, 'Isn't this wonderful?' . . . He saw this exciting, cataclysmic drama in the ordinary."

In fact, Shepherd saw his popularity surge while at WOR largely because of his "ordinary" sensibilities. His radio show broadcasted regularly on weeknights between 1 a.m. and 5:30 a.m., and he didn't use a script or notes. He spoke on the radio like an elder around a campfire telling stories to his kin. His stories explored the simple aspects of life, often with many diversions, extraneous adjectives and adverbs, and convoluted plot twists that added more flair to the story.

Shepherd occasionally told semi-autobiographical stories about his "Old Man," Jean Parker Shepherd Sr., his mother, Ann, and Randy, his kid brother. He often assumed the role of a character named Ralphie, whose life experiences closely mirrored his own. Stories about his childhood were communicated through the fictional Parker family, also of Hammond. In 1964, his stories started to appear in *Playboy* (for those who read the magazine for the articles). In 1966, Shep released an anthology of Ralphie's stories, *In God We Trust, All Others Pay Cash*, which became a runaway hit and, to this day, has never been out of print.

As Bob Clark listened to the radio broadcast that day, he couldn't help but be reminded of his own upbringing. He was born on August 3, 1939, in New Orleans, but his family moved to Birmingham, Alabama, soon after. Shep's stories reflected Midwestern values and a certain simple charm that had long since been lost by the 1960s, but as Clark realized while he was listening, and as thousands of other listeners nationwide already had discovered, the values typically described as "Midwestern" are hardly specific to that region of the United States. Sure, Clark had probably never experienced a snow storm in Alabama, and certainly not at the University of Miami, where he attended school for Creative Dramatic Writing after reneging on his acceptance of a football scholarship at Hillsdale College in Michigan, but there isn't a child in the country who didn't wish against the odds for something they wanted for Christmas, even though their parents told them it was not likely to materialize under the tree on December 25.

Clark's career had yet to take off. He was a student working on making a name for himself directing regional theater in the Miami area. A local film producer suggested to him that he might want to take a crack at directing for the screen. He accepted, and in 1966, *The Emperor's New Clothes*, a short film starring none other than Hollywood icon John Carradine, became Clark's directorial debut.

A year later, Clark spearheaded a project called *She-Man*, a short film about a soldier who is blackmailed to take estrogen pills and wear lingerie by a sadistic transvestite. Listening to the radio the evening he was to pick up his date, the young director decided what his first feature film project would be. He stopped taxiing around the neighborhood and arrived at his destination, just short of an hour late.

"I picked up my very irate date," Clark recalled. "And I decided at that moment that I was going to make a movie of Jean's work."

What was it about Shep's storytelling that had made such an impression on Clark?

"I was so enamored with his offhand, flippant kind of deceptively wry and witty comments," Clark said.

However, the road to the Cineplex was harder than the young director had anticipated. He had hoped *A Christmas Story* would be his first feature film, and strongly believing it would be a success, he began work on a script even before gaining Shep's participation and approval.

But *A Christmas Story* wasn't Clark's first feature. Instead, he directed a series of horror films throughout the 1970s, including *Children Shouldn't Play with Dead Things*, *Dead of Night*, and his first seasonal flick, *Black Christmas*. During this time, Clark reached out to Jean with the offer to help bring his stories to film. The storyteller, whose stories were now appearing weekly on television in a PBS series entitled *Jean Shepherd's America*, was ecstatic.

Fred Barzyk, *America*'s producer, remembers Shep's initial excitement. "[Bob Clark] was another of these kinds of people who were drawn deeply to Shepherd," he says. "And he came to Shepherd and said, 'I want to do *A Christmas Story*,' and for Shepherd this was big because it was going to be a movie. Maybe at long last people would recognize Shepherd as an important American icon. So he cut off all things with television. Didn't invite me to the set, he didn't do anything. He had moved on."

But the move wouldn't be immediate. Before the movie could be shopped around to studio executives, it had to be written. It was agreed that Shepherd would write the script, which would be a composite of his published short stories, most of which appeared in his 1966 anthology *In God We Trust*, and unpublished tales from his appearances at colleges throughout the 1970s. Leigh Brown, Shep's wife and longtime producer, would cowrite, along with Bob Clark himself.

"It substantially comes from Shepherd's work except, oddly enough, the narration," the director said in 2003 about the screenplay. "We probably worked the narration more because we had to fit various pieces."

One of the aspects of the film that sets it apart from others of the time is Shep's narration, which is both intellectual and simplistic. At times, the voice-over, which Shepherd himself provided in the voice of Ralphie as an adult, serves to comment on what the young protagonist was thinking at the time of the film's events. In other cases, adult Ralphie uses the narration as an opportunity to comment on what occurred in his family after the film's events, as a way of showing the importance of this time period in the Parkers' lives.

Whether the filmmakers knew this at the time is uncertain, but the narration ended up being an essential component of the movie, as it serves as a bridge between the adult world and the kid world. The young, and young at heart, can appreciate the insight into little Ralphie's thoughts, which often cause the audience to recall their own childhood antics. Additionally, grown-ups watching the movie see the narration as a vehicle by which to appreciate the nostalgia in the film. *A Christmas Story* is as much about being a child in the 1940s as it is about how times have changed since then. Jean Shepherd, with his familiarly sardonic voice and his uniquely witty critique on situations, takes us through that journey with his disembodied performance in the film.

Of course, the movie isn't simply about how things have changed since the post-Depression era. As the French novelist Jean-Baptiste Alphonse Karr wrote in 1849, "The more things change, the more they stay the same." This is certainly one of the themes present in *A Christmas Story*. While kids in the 1980s weren't racing home to listen to *Little Orphan Annie* on the radio, they were bolting from school to catch episodes of their favorite shows on television. Little brothers were still annoying; parents still argued and didn't understand their kids. The timelessness of the film is more important than the fact that it is set in a particular era in American history.

This agelessness is one of the true accomplishments of Shepherd's work, in spite of its contemporary references. For example, Ralphie doesn't long for any old toy weapon but instead a Red Ryder BB gun "with a compass in the stock and this thing that tells time." One needs only to have seen the film or an advertisement for a Red Ryder BB gun once to see this specific model in their imagination, which is astonishing, especially since this toy never actually existed. It was merely a creation of Shepherd's fantastic mind. In recent years the gun has been available for sale as a result of the film's enduring popularity. Despite this truth, the reference to that particular toy, as well as the evocation of *Little Orphan Annie* radio serials, *The Wizard of Oz*, and, in the original short story, *Snow White and the Seven Dwarfs*, still manages to induce a nostalgic feeling and yearning for "the good old days," even for those who weren't around during that period. Shep's work doesn't feel dated because of the references — it simultaneously feels classic and timeless.

As a testament to just how timeless Shep's stories are, exactly when *A Christmas Story* is set remains ambiguous. In 2003, Bob Clark stated that the film wasn't set in a specific year. Instead, it takes place sometime between

Melinda Dillon and Ian Petrella © Ian Petrella

the late 1930s and early 1940s. Props in the film corroborate this. The *Look Magazine* with Shirley Temple on the cover, where Ralphie slips in an advertisement for his mother to see, is from 1937; however, the Speed-O-Matic style decoder he receives wasn't released until 1940.

In the end, the inconsistencies as to which Christmas season the film chronicles almost make the movie more realistic. After all, the film is a flashback, and as every adult knows, childhood memories can sometimes become distorted. The adult Ralphie narrator in the movie may be unreliable regarding the specific details, but what's important is his overall impression of his quest to obtain what he describes as "the greatest Christmas gift I had ever received, or would ever receive."

For the main framework of the film, it was decided to use "Duel in the Snow, or, Red Ryder Nails the Cleveland Street Kid," which first appeared in *Playboy* in 1964. The story was part of *In God We Trust* two years later. The central plot is all too familiar for any fan of the film: Ralphie Parker wants nothing more than to find an Official Red Ryder Carbine Action Two-Hundred-Shot Range Model Air Rifle under his Christmas tree.

A great deal of "Duel in the Snow" materializes in the finished film. Besides the primary story arc, there are minor details that found their way into the script. Ralphie's teacher makes an appearance, even though her name, Miss Bodkin, was changed to Miss Shields. Our hero receives pink bunny slippers from Aunt Clara, but with the goal of going for the deeper belly laugh, the screenwriting trio changed the footwear into a full-fledged outfit that made Ralphie look like "a deranged Easter bunny." In a self-deprecating touch, Jean Shepherd had written the pajama joke in homage to his real-life frustrations with being given a girl's name. He would often tell of how he had to beat kids up who teased him about his name — Jean with a "J" — when he was a youngster. When Ralphie says in the film that he's convinced his aunt thought he was a girl all his life, it's a more autobiographical moment of Shepherd than some might realize.

Die-hard fans will notice other consistencies between the story and the film. In the short story, Ralphie describes the process of getting ready for school as being "like getting ready for extended Deep-Sea Diving," a line echoed in the film. The boys attend Warren G. Harding Elementary School, the real location of Shepherd's elementary education, in both the story and the film. The enterprising Ralphie also sneaks advertisements for the gun between the pages of his mother's magazines, in an attempt to remind her about his Christmas wish, and the Old Man has tantrums filled with four-letter words directed at the cantankerous furnace in the basement.

In reading Shep's original short stories, what sticks out is how he celebrates aspects of life that most people would consider unworthy of celebrating. The casual dinnertime ritual between parents and children facilitates deep character studies, filled as it is with interpersonal drama and cerebral passages about such mundane concepts like the temperature of the cabbage on the plate or whether or not the oldest son said a bad word at school that day. This is, of course, to say that Jean Shepherd had a natural knack for writing about life as it is and, in many ways, as it used to be. For him, the past was not only a prologue but also the present.

"He talked about the traditional minor pleasures of growing up and he depicts typical family life and their relationships," says Eugene B. Bergmann, author of *Excelsior, You Fathead! The Art and Enigma of Jean Shepherd*. "The kind mother, the annoying kid brother, the father who's a bit distant and stern, but who comes through in the end with a present Ralphie wants so badly.

"He made a lot of comments about 'Gee, look, this is the way people actually act,'" Bergmann continues. "What he liked to say is that people are full of what he would describe as 'foibles,' and that doesn't mean horrible characteristics, just sort of a little bit of humor and caring and love for humanity in the imperfections that he found for people. He liked to describe those strange things people would sometimes do and he would like to suggest that they were both not quite the way an intelligent person should act, and yet they were amusing and loveable also. I found that rather touching and always funny."

Jean Shepherd's love for the ordinary was also apparent in the other stories that informed the film's script. "The Counterfeit Secret Circle Member Gets the Message, or, The Asp Strikes Again," a story that appeared for the first time in *In God We Trust*, was also influential. The short story finds Ralphie frenzied after his *Little Orphan Annie* secret decoder pin arrives in the mail and he sets out to decipher the encrypted message that was delivered in a series of letters and number combinations. The story ends with the message turning out to be nothing more than "a crummy commercial" for Ovaltine. In 1965's "Grover Dill and the Tasmanian Devil," which was originally published by *Playboy* and later turned up in *In God We Trust*, Shepherd follows the neighborhood bully and one of his toadies as they target their next victim. This story also ended up being interwoven into the fabric of the film's script in a scene that taught the world that Lifebuoy soap tasted disgusting and could even lead to blindness as a result of "soap poisoning." The resolution to this story was incorporated into the sequence of the film; it occurs after Ralphie utters "the queen-mother of all dirty words," a significant change from the original short story it was lifted from.

Based on the success of *In God We Trust*, in 1971 Shepherd released a second short story anthology entitled *Wanda Hickey's Night of Golden Memories: And Other Disasters*. It is in that collection that "The Grandstand Passion Play of Delbert and the Bumpus Hounds" appears. There are noticeable influences from "Passion Play" on the final script, but fans of the film will notice some substantial differences. For example, in *A Christmas Story*, the meal that is taken from the Parker home isn't ham, but turkey. More importantly, the original short story isn't even set around Christmastime, but Easter. Very little of the story actually materializes in the film, except for the Old Man's adverse relationship with the redneck family which, in the movie, is only referenced.

It's safe to say that when the narratives were raided for stories that would be a perfect fit for the silver screen, even Jean Shepherd himself couldn't have anticipated the importance of including "My Old Man and the Lascivious Special Award That Heralded the Birth of Pop Art," which appeared for the first time in *In God We Trust*. The now all-too-familiar story is the tale of Ralphie's father, who wins a "major award" in the form of a distinctive lamp, ". . . a silk-stockinged lady's leg, realistically flesh-colored, wearing a black spike-heeled slipper," Shepherd wrote. "The knee was crooked slightly and the leg was shown to the middle of the thigh. That was all. No face; no torso; no dress — just a stark, disembodied, provocative leg."

It is here that Shep's unique storytelling ability is best displayed. After the mother breaks her husband's prized possession, the patriarch's response is not only completely in line with what we would expect from the character but also the kind of resolution longtime fans of the raconteur came to love from his undeniably humorous stories.

"My father always was a superb user of profanity," Shepherd wrote in the story. "But now he came out with just one word, a real Father word, bitter and hard.

"'Dammit.'"

Molded in the pre-television era of radio serials, Jean Shepherd was a walking, talking, and almost always monologuing relic. He had made a name for himself by speaking for hours on end into a radio microphone, virtually isolating himself. When callers were encouraged to call his radio broadcast, Shep would often refuse to pick up the phone. Instead, he would talk to himself, making up voices and pretending he was arguing with real callers. While touring the college circuit on speaking engagements, he would berate students who called out from the crowd and remind them that he was performing a solo act and shouldn't be disturbed. Those who interviewed him on television and radio found him to be an enigma. His stories contradicted anecdotes he had previously told and he would claim that he was telling the truth both times, while also laughing at the suggestion that anyone actually believed him.

Although Shepherd regularly used the phrase "I'll never forget the time" to begin a story, an obvious attempt to lend some truth to his wildly exaggerated, or downright fabricated, stories, he simultaneously maintained that his tales were simply a work of fiction and nothing more. That is, unless he was saying the opposite.

"I take people out of my past or I put them and use them as composite characters just as any good writer would," Shep said at Fairleigh Dickinson University in 1967. "You don't write out of a vacuum. I used real names, but they're not exactly like they are in the stories."

"None of these stories, by the way, are based on any of my own memories," he stated in a 1975 interview with Barry Farber on WOR. "None of them are based on any — the families are all — I've created a mythical family, like Faulkner created a mythical county."

So, which is true? Are Flick and Schwartz actual people, or merely creations of Jean Shepherd's imagination? The question seems to be one that Shep not only invited but relished.

"Although he told hundreds of stories about his kidhood, the extent to which the tales were true to the 'real' Jean Shepherd is difficult to discern," author Eugene B. Bergmann writes in his book on Shepherd. "His adolescence is almost a blank record."

Despite his repeated declarations that his stories were all made up, there *was* a real Flick — Jack Flickinger — who lived just a few blocks away from

the Shepherds. Miss Ruth Shields was really one of young Jean's teachers, and there was even a family from Kentucky who lived next door.

At best, Shep's claims to have fabricated all the stories about his friends and family seem to be a gross misremembering of the truth. Shep did have a younger brother named Randall. In his stories, Randy was a fairly boiler-plate younger brother: there were the occasional displays of sibling rivalry that would result in a play-fight, or the younger would be engaged in some display of immaturity, like refusing to eat his food at the dinner table, making a mess and refusing to clean it up, or hiding in kitchen cupboards. When Shep moved away from Hammond, the real Randy stayed behind, working for the Borden Milk Company until his adulthood.

There is no evidence to suggest that Randy was as annoying as Shepherd wrote, but in a way, this potential inconsistency hits at the heart of what made his writing such a success. Through his alter ego of Ralphie Parker, the adult Shepherd wrote about his kid brother in the way that he viewed Randy when he was younger. What pair of brothers, as youngsters, especially those as close in age as the Parker/Shepherd pair, would take the time to get to know the other as a person and not just "my older brother" or "my kid brother"? In Randy's ambiguity there is a truth that resonates strongly with Shep's audience, mostly because it allows for the nondescript younger brother to serve as a blank slate for the immature and annoying elementary school–aged family member in each of our lives.

In his stories, the mother is always portrayed as a plain-looking and slightly pathetic character, certainly not quite ready for someone to drop by unexpectedly, for she was likely to be in her chenille bathrobe with some stain on it that she had chosen to ignore because she had no one to impress. The mother meant well, as most do, but wouldn't parent in the traditional sense. Shep would often tell a story of his mother sitting him on her knee, extolling about the virtues of money making as the key to success in life. Having an honest job that enables you to pay your way in life is a valuable thing to aspire to, but most mothers wouldn't consider that the best lesson to teach a child at an early age. In her eyes, money wasn't the root of all evil; it was the ticket to happiness. The child Shepherd accepted his mother's wisdom, but as an adult, he recognized that his mother's advice prematurely turned him into a somewhat hardened cynic who rejected that anyone should sacrifice making money to create art.

"Jean, you got to make dough," Shepherd claims his mother would tell him when he was five years old. "You got to make dough."

So, throughout his life, that's what he set out to do.

And what of his father, the one that audiences remember as the inaccessible, yet good-at-heart white knight that ultimately gets Ralphie the Red Ryder bb gun he so desired? How accurate is his portrayal in the film to Jean Shepherd's real Old Man?

While the script written by the trio of collaborators portrays the father, the Old Man, as a blue-collar family man with a hard exterior, it seems that this was a departure from not only the father Shep often wrote about in his stories but also the man he lived with until adulthood.

First off, the Shepherds weren't blue-collar. The real-life Old Man worked for a milk company as a cashier, the same company where the real-life Randy worked. While the film suggests that the Parkers are working class, a lot of the original stories that inspired the movie actually deal with the juxtaposition of being a family of modest means living in a steel mill city in industrial Indiana.

Additionally, the softer side of the father that appears at moments like when he buys Ralphie the Red Ryder bb gun may not have actually existed.

If it did, it certainly isn't how Shepherd actually remembered his father.

"He never offered much advice, my father," he recalled in April 1960. "He never really offered any advice that I can pull out of the great — I'm always amused — not only amused, I'm always a little bit — I feel a little inferior. These guys I read all the time who write autobiographies and it seems that people were always saying great things to them that affected their lives."

In his book on Jean Shepherd, Eugene B. Bergmann cites the source of what Shep himself described as hatred for his father. Shep had asked actor James Broderick, who played the Old Man in the 1976 television movie *The Phantom of the Open Hearth*, to predict what happened after the events of the film ended, and then let the actor in on the answer.

"Okay," Shep began. "One year to the day after Ralph's prom, in fact the week of Ralph's high school graduation, the Old Man comes home, announces he's leaving the family, and takes off for Palm Beach with a twenty-year-old stenographer with long blond hair and a Ford convertible. They never hear from him again."

This wasn't just Shepherd trying to convince the actor to delve deeper into the part; it was his art imitating life. "I think it was one of the major blows in Shepherd's life, why he had such a damaged ego in many ways," producer Fred Barzyk says. "Everybody reacts differently to different kinds of losses. When his father sat him down and said he's [sic] leaving his mother, it really — it was real pain for Shepherd."

Characteristic of Jean Shepherd's usual frankness but somewhat surprising for promotional materials in advance of a film's release, MGM's production notes for the film provided some insight into the raconteur's true feelings about not only his real parents but also the way Ralphie's parents appear in the film.

"I saw the Old Man in *A Christmas Story* as a guy who grew up hustling pool games at the age of twelve and was supporting himself by the age of fourteen," Shepherd was reported as saying in 1983. "And Darren McGavin's sardonic attitude was exactly the characterization I had in mind. Ralphie's mother is the kind of woman I figure grew up in a family of four or five sisters and married young. She digs the Old Man, but also knows he's as dangerous as a snake. In a way, the movie is really about these people, not Christmas or Santa Claus."

According to Scott Schwartz, the actor cast as Flick in the film, the screenwriting process consisted primarily of taking Shepherd's stories and making them more simplistic for a general audience. "Jean Shepherd had a vocabulary second to none," Schwartz says. "You could hand him a ball-point pen and he could describe you for a half an hour. His vocabulary was out of this world. When they wrote *A Christmas Story*, they really had to tone down a lot of his vocabulary to more laymen's terms so that everybody could understand it."

The script was completed six months after they began working on it and, to the disappointment of all involved in the writing process, nothing else happened with it. Clark attempted to drum up some interest from movie studios to produce the film, but because he was a director with some modest B-movie hits underneath his belt, no executives were very warm to the idea of having him spearhead a quaint Christmas movie set in the Depression era. The idea, they were sure, wouldn't resonate with audiences, and there was nothing in Clark's resumé that suggested to them that he could take a film that sounded like it had a snowball's chance in hell of being successful.

And then he directed a little film called *Porky's*. In 1982, you were hard pressed to find a film critic of significance saying anything kind about the raunchy teen comedy. Celebrated movie appraiser Roger Ebert of the *Chicago Sun-Times* gave the film one-and-a-half stars, easily one of the more positive reviews, and stated that Bob Clark "blew it" when it came to making a good film. He concluded his review with one final dig: "I see that I have neglected to summarize the plot of *Porky's*. And I don't think I will," he wrote. "I don't feel like writing one more sentence (which is, to be sure, all it would take)."

As Ebert's review, which uses three sentences to state that it won't waste one more on providing context to his opinion piece, demonstrated, Bob Clark's film was one that critics loved to hate. However, despite the vitriol from the chattering class, or perhaps because of it, teenagers lined up around the block to see it. The movie, which was produced for $5 million, made over $105 million in its initial theatrical run and was the fifth highest grossing film

Bob Clark on the set of *Porky's* © Twentieth Century Fox Film Corporation / Photofest

of the year in the United States, behind *E.T.: The Extra-Terrestrial*, *Tootsie*, *An Officer and a Gentleman*, and *Rocky III*. In short, it was a mammoth success, and as mammoth successes often do in the film industry, it gave Clark some capital to spend — and he knew just the project to spend it on.

"*Porky's* has allowed me to make studio films without having to sacrifice any of the freedom or control I had as an independent," he said in 1983. "At an earlier stage, I would have been forced to make unacceptable creative compromises — but not now."

A Christmas Story, which at the time was still being referred to under the working title *In God We Trust* as a nod to Shepherd's original collection of short stories, was re-pitched to the major motion pictures studios. After much persuasion, MGM agreed to give Clark $4.4 million to produce the film. To save money, Clark agreed to work on the film without a fee, and even contributed $150,000 of his own money to the production. It was later reported that as a result, the director was made a forty percent stakeholder in the film. Those familiar with Jean Shepherd's business dealings claim that he also contributed financially to the film and was part owner, but the details are less clear.

As happy as the director was to finally be making *A Christmas Story*, the experience was often bittersweet for him. Although a major studio agreed to release the film, they had no expectations that it would be successful and

Director Bob Clark with Peter Billingsley, Melinda Dillon, Ian Petrella, and Darren McGavin © Ian Petrella little faith that it would even be worth watching. They provided such a small budget and so little support that what should have been Clark's blessing was, at times, perceived to be a bit of a curse.

"I've paid a terrible price to do this picture," he said in March of 1983, as filming was wrapping in Toronto. "I have to do three films back-to-back this year. I'm a bonded slave right now. I like the material in each one of them. But they [Hollywood studios] play very hard ball. But I will never have to do that again. However, I'm sure whatever I want to do the next time, they'll extract a very high price from me.

"I said I wouldn't work [on another film] until I do [*A Christmas Story*]," he continued. "So I'm doing *A Christmas Story* as part of a package for MGM. And I have a two-picture deal with Fox, although they let me off to do this one."

A production company, Christmas Tree Films, was established through the collaboration of Clark and Shepherd, and while post-production was being completed on the inevitable *Porky's* sequel, they began to move full steam ahead on making the film that Clark had paid his high price for. If MGM had known the film was going to be a success, perhaps they would have thrown more money at the picture. For Clark's crew and the cast, the process of moviemaking might have been a little bit easier, but then, without the need for some creative cost-cutting throughout shooting, the whole thing might have been a lot less fun and the final film a lot less charming.

Filling the role of Ralphie, the film's pint-sized protagonist, was relatively easy. By the time he auditioned for *A Christmas Story*, Peter Billingsley was already a recognizable face to the public. He had scored his first television commercial gig at the age of two and appeared in over a hundred commercials before he was a teenager. Messy Marvin, a pseudo-spokesman for Hershey's chocolate syrup, was one of his most memorable characters.

Billingsley's work wasn't limited to commercials. In 1981, he starred alongside Burt Reynolds in the film *Paternity*, which earned him a nomination in the "Best Young Comedian — Motion Picture or Television" category at the Young Artist Awards. The following year he was nominated in the same category for his stint co-hosting the NBC series *Real People*.

So it was a mild surprise to him that after he auditioned for *A Christmas Story*, he went weeks without hearing back from his agent as to whether or not he had gotten the role. Billingsley was the first actor who was seriously considered for the part, but director Bob Clark passed him over because he thought the choice was too obvious. A nationwide search ensued, which resulted in over 8,000 kids auditioning for the lead role. Ultimately, Clark came to his senses. He watched Billingsley's audition tape again and made his decision that instant. "I must be crazy," the director said out loud to himself. "Peter *is* Ralphie."

The decision to cast Billingsley was a smart one. Not only was the actor perfect on-screen, but he also was the consummate professional on the set. By the time the film was released, the promotional team at MGM was so impressed with his poise and intelligence that they boasted his 150 IQ score in press materials for the film. Other *Christmas Story* alum who shared the screen with him sing his praises to this day.

© Ian Petrella

"Peter Billingsley was gifted like Jackie Cooper, Shirley Temple, and some of the great kid actors from the past," says Tedde Moore, who played his schoolteacher, Miss Shields. "He was the most terrific boy. He worked very hard and understood what he was doing and loved it. It was like he wasn't a child."

"I was excited to work with Peter Billingsley because I was a big fan of *Real People* and his Hershey commercials," says Zack Ward, who played Ralphie's main tormentor, the yellow-eyed Scut Farkus. "I was a little star-struck by him."

"I knew exactly who he was, so it was kind of exciting working with him," says Ian Petrella, who was cast as the kid brother Randy. "We developed a friendship, but it was obvious we kind of had this older brother–little brother thing going on where we got along, but then there'd be times where we didn't get along. That's just how kids are. We got along really well, though. It was a great experience working with him."

Melinda Dillon was cast as the matriarch to the Parker family, primarily based on her appearance in *Close Encounters of the Third Kind*. According to Bob Clark, she was the only person seriously considered for the role. "*Close*

Melinda Dillon with
Ian Petrella and
Peter Billingsley
© Ian Petrella

Encounters was all I needed to see," he said. "I talked to her and she wanted to do it, so we did it."

On the set, Dillon was the big superstar as far as the kids were concerned. Her young co-stars, especially Ian Petrella, idolized her. "Melinda was an absolute sweetheart," he explains. "At the same time, she marked my first time working with a celebrity. She was the mother in *Close Encounters of the Third Kind*, and that was one of my favorite films growing up. I got to work with someone who worked with aliens, so that was pretty awesome. I had a lot of questions for her about it — 'How did they make the aliens? How did they get them to move?' She was just very kind and very sweet about all of that. We got along great. She was wonderful to everybody. She was wonderful to my mom and wonderful to all the kids."

Veteran character actor Darren McGavin was cast as Frank Parker, although in the film he is simply referred to as "the Old Man." The actor played the title role in the television series *Kolchak: The Night Stalker*, and alongside Burt Reynolds in the NBC western series *Riverboat*. By the time he appeared on screen as the grumpy head of the Parker clan, he was a recognizable face to many in the viewing audience.

While it seems as though the actor was born to play the Old Man, the part nearly went to an even more famous Hollywood hotshot. Jack Nicholson, who had already won an Academy Award for *One Flew Over the Cuckoo's Nest*, initially expressed interest in being a part of the film.

"I had gone to meet with Jack," director Bob Clark said in 2003. "They wanted me to do a film with Jack called *Turn Left or Die* at MGM, but they also gave Jack the script to *A Christmas Story*. They didn't tell me until later that Jack really liked *A Christmas Story* and might very well have done it, but they didn't want to pay Jack Nicholson money to do *A Christmas Story*."

According to Clark, McGavin was aware that he wasn't the first choice for the role, and made it a priority to show that he was deserving and appreciative of it. "He knew full well there had been at least four other actors projected [for this part]," Clark says. "When I met him off the plane, he said, 'Who's the person who had sense enough to put me in this part?' and I was able to say, 'Me,' because I was asking for him from the first over some of the bigger name actors."

In the end, everything worked out the way it should have. Nicholson went on to film *Terms of Endearment*, which earned him his second Academy Award, and McGavin went on to star in what would become the most recognizable role of his career.

"Jack is fabulous," Clark said. "I love him, but thank God he didn't [end up with the part] because Darren *is* the Old Man."

The other actors in the film concur. Not only is McGavin impressive on-screen, but he also left a lasting impression on the other performers he worked with on the film. "Darren was professional," Petrella says. "He was definitely a nice guy, but I didn't know that before starting the film. I didn't know much about Darren and who he was, but my mom did. One of the things she told me was that a lot of times, older actors don't necessarily like to work with younger actors, 'so let's not find out the hard way and let's just be on our best behav-

ior around Mr. McGavin.' And that's what I was. I was on my best behavior around him. And I think because of that, there are no bad stories to tell."

Despite his early trepidations and his mother's warning, Ian found the actor great to work with. McGavin's level of professionalism extended beyond his performance, as the actor also showed a concern for the production aspects of the film. "He had a lot of vested interest in this film, so it was just as important to him to make sure this was a good movie as it was for Bob and it was for Jean," Petrella continues. "When Darren was on the set, he was ready to go and do his part. He probably wasn't going to put up with the antics of an eight-year-old, so I made sure that he didn't have to."

"Darren was great," Peter Billingsley said in 2003. "I had never worked with someone who knew so much about everything. Any question

Darren McGavin in *Kolchak: The Night Stalker*
© Universal TV / Photofest

Ian Petrella
© Ian Petrella

on the set, Darren had faced it. He had been through it. He had been through it. He was such a pro and didn't have to tell you that he was. He was just so confident and knew absolutely everything." Tedde Moore agrees: "He was a really beautifully trained actor, a really serious actor."

Ian Petrella was the last child to be hired for *A Christmas Story*. Prior to shooting, the cast members rehearsed for the film at director Bob Clark's house in Canada, but without the character of kid brother Randy. While McGavin, Dillon, and Billingsley prepared, and with just a few days left before shooting was to begin, an aggressive search was going on behind the scenes to find the last piece of the Parker family puzzle.

"I was a child actor and it was just another random audition that you go out for," Ian explains. "My agent called me up and said I was needed to fill the role of the younger brother in a holiday film and that was pretty much it."

With Clark and his crew relieved that they would start shooting on schedule, Ian was also excited to be cast in his first feature film. "I was a big fan of films at a young age," he says. "So, not only did I value that I was going to be in a movie, but I also was going to get to see how movies were made." *A Christmas Story* was an excellent film for him to cut his teeth on. Bob Clark was supportive and, for the young actor, it was generally fun to have the freedom to be a kid.

"Bob Clark allowed you as a child to bring in certain moments of your life to your performance," he says. "Randy wasn't a specific character. For God's sake, he had all of three lines in the film. He's basically the R2-D2 of *A Christmas Story*. He makes funny noises, whines and cries, and laughs and falls in the snow so there wasn't a whole lot to him. Everything was physicality with Randy, and as far as Bob was concerned, there wasn't this whole backstory on who Randy was. We didn't have conversations like what were his dreams, what were his visions . . . he's a frickin' kid! He doesn't want to eat his food and that's it."

With the principal cast in place, production moved forward. While the film was set in Hohman, a fictitious city based on Hammond, Indiana, where Jean Shepherd grew up, Cleveland was decided as the first shooting location.

This was mostly due to a little department store named Higbee's, and the owners' unprecedented desire to transform their store into the North Pole.

CHAPTER TWO

Atop Mighty
Mount Olympus

A **half-mile away** from Higbee's department store, in the suburbs of Cleveland Heights, Patty Johnson came home after a long day of teaching. Her two young children were looking forward to eating, and their mother, exasperated from her day of having been with other people's young children, was not looking forward to cooking. Reluctantly, she went to the kitchen, took out a pot, and just as she set it on the stove, the phone rang.

"Patty?" the voice said.

Higbee's as it appears
in *A Christmas Story*
© Reuben Freed

"Yes," she answered.

"This is Karen Fields," the voice answered. "I have a great opportunity for you, an audition. A movie is being shot in Cleveland and you have to come down and audition for it!"

There was a pause on the line. Patty heard her children arguing. She thought about her long day and the one yet to come tomorrow. She thought about how she was late in making their dinner and how she wasn't in the mood to fight for them to eat their vegetables for a third consecutive night.

"Karen, honey," Patty said to the agent. "I have work tomorrow." There was another pause on the line. "You know I'd love to, but I . . ."

"Patty, you've gotta come in."

Before becoming a schoolteacher and mother, Patty Johnson made the rounds as an actress. She signed up with David & Lee, a Cleveland-based modeling agency, but before long, the agency had expanded to represent acting talent as well. Patty, who already was a veteran of local theater, took gigs with PlayhouseSquare, a theater group in town, and other professional work.

But as often happens, she felt it was time to grow up and get a "real job." She became certified to teach and had two children. She settled down and pushed acting aside, until the agency came around to pull her back in.

The idea of auditioning for a feature film was intriguing to Patty, of course, but there were more significant problems than her work schedule. The phone call arrived on a Monday evening, two days after she had buried her mother, who had passed away the week before. She had already missed several days of work and, more importantly, the former actress wasn't certain she was in the mental state to jump back in with both feet.

"I really don't know if I have the flexibility in my schedule right now," she said.

"It's a really great role," Karen said. "It has a Screen Actors Guild contract attached to it. They're looking for an elf with a really bad attitude and I have a feeling you'll get it!"

Patty didn't know whether to be flattered or offended, but she made a decision. She was going to jump. "I can't wait and languish in line," Patty thought out loud. "The best I can do is come by and audition during my lunch break. I can run downtown, but you have to be able to get me in and get me out. If you can promise me that, I'd be happy to do it."

The next day began as the one that preceded it, except Patty, who normally skipped breakfast, decided to eat something since she would be forgoing lunch. She went through the first half of her day and, when the bell sounded at the appropriate time, she raced to the door and made her way over to the audition.

Dozens of girls filled the lobby of the audition hall, waiting for their turn to be seen. As instructed, Patty made her way to the casting agents' office and knocked on the glass window. The door opened and the icy stares from her competitors who were left behind pierced through her back. She made her way in to meet with Ken Goch, the first assistant director, who was spearheading the casting for the Cleveland-based actors.

She was given a piece of script, which is known in the business as a "side," and was told to deliver the lines in her most convincing evil-elf interpretation. She felt she had nailed it, but just for added security, she brought out her secret weapon. She reached into her bag, pulled out five Polaroid pictures, and handed them to the casting director.

"You see," she said. "Not only am I an actress, but I also have experience — elf experience!"

The assistant director looked at the pictures. Patty, dressed as an elf, was in Higbee's performing as a singing elf, a side gig she'd worked a few years earlier while she was doing a show at PlayhouseSquare. She was sure she had sealed the deal now.

He thumbed through the pictures, periodically looking at Patty and comparing the person in front of him to the smiling woman in green tights and booties in the pictures.

"You know, you have a lot of qualities that the director is looking for," Goch started hesitantly. "I'm not sure if they told you, but his concept is really to cast a teenager in this role."

The thirty-two-year-old's stomach rumbled as she stared back at the casting director. She thought about how long it had been since she had eaten, how she'd raced out the door, had virtually climbed over a bunch of jealous actresses waiting outside. She was sure she'd have to do that again on her way back to her car. She thought about how her gut had told her she shouldn't go to the stupid audition in the first place. She thought about how stressful and emotional the previous week had been, and how she was getting stressed all over again.

She stared at him, and then the former elf got angry.

"You mean to tell me," she started, "that I dragged my ass all the way down here when you wanted a *teenager*?"

"Well, yes, but—"

"Don't you know my credentials? If you wanted a *teenager*, you really needed to be clearer in your casting notice, don'tcha think? You know what, good luck with your *teenagers*, but if you want a professional actress, you know where I am!"

She snatched the photos out of his hand, headed toward the door, but turned back around with one final retort.

"Have a merry Christmas!"

She pushed through the piles of women waiting on the floor outside the room and made her way back to her car, incensed over what had just happened.

"I can't wait to give Karen a call when I get off work," she thought. *"She is going to get a piece of my mind! She needs to ask better questions. This was so stupid!"*

When she arrived home, she could hear her phone ringing inside as she put the key in the door.

"Hello, Patty?" It was Karen. "I've been trying to reach you for hours! You've got to—"

"You've got to be more careful when you make people waste their lunch break on illegitimate auditions," she snapped.

"Illegitimate auditions?" Karen was confused, but she continued. "They want you to go down and have a second audition. They loved you! The director is flying in tonight and they want you to meet him."

Ian Petrella and
Patty Johnson
© Ian Petrella

Patty just stood there. "Look, there must be some mistake," she said. "Do you know what happened when I went down there?"

As it turned out, the agent didn't know, so for the next few minutes, she was treated to an emotional recreation of the story from soup to nuts.

"I'm sure they made a mistake," Patty concluded.

"I don't know about all that, but they want you. They were quite clear. They want you to go down tomorrow for a second interview."

Patty decided to return the next day and scribbled the details on the back of a crumpled-up receipt she found in her pocket. The next day, like the one before, she returned to the same location during her lunch break, but instead of being faced with dozens of girls when she reached her destination, this time just one stood in front of her. Patty inhaled and exhaled deeply as she sized up the girl. She was young. She was pretty. She was a *teenager.*

"Well, this could be ugly," Patty thought, but she had gotten this far, so there was nothing left to do but stick it out and see what happened.

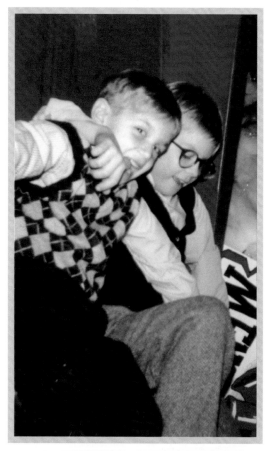

Ian Petrella and Peter Billingsley © Ian Petrella

They called her in and she met director Bob Clark. They chatted for a few minutes. Patty waited for a script, but it never came, and neither did the second audition.

"We're definitely going with you," the director said as he shook her hand. "We're sending you down to wardrobe now for a fitting."

In the walk down to the costumer, the actress was told what she had suspected: her tantrum at the initial casting call had sealed the deal. She was silently giddy as she realized that she had just landed her first major motion picture screen credit, something that was certain to boost her acting resumé.

The shoot started a week later, and seemed to be unending. "It seemed like we were there for forty days and forty nights," she jokes.

In reality, it lasted only a week in January. Reuben Freed, the film's production designer, oversaw the transformation of Higbee's into a retro winter wonderland housed inside of a department store. A thirty-foot-tall platform was erected, which the cast and crew took to affectionately calling Mount Olympus, with a large slide to discard the children after they had their opportunity to meet Santa Claus. A colossal staircase was built to aid in the elves' ascent. According to the film's production notes, the project took twelve men three weeks to construct.

As time-consuming as it was to get the inside of the department store to travel back in time, the outside of Higbee's was left virtually untouched. When looking for a city in the United States that could pass as a 1940s Midwestern town, Bob Clark sent scouts to twenty different locations. Cleveland quickly emerged as the choice, primarily because of the family-owned department store.

Higbee's was a small store founded in 1860, but in the early 1930s, it moved downtown into a massive complex called Terminal Tower. The building was largely unchanged over the following fifty years. Outside, a large neon sign adorned the building's retro façade. Inside, large crystal chandeliers hung on the main floor and a narrow wooden escalator took customers upstairs. The doors were all made of brass with art deco designs, and the display cases were trimmed in a wood finish. In other words, it was perfect.

While the store didn't appear to be a year older than 1933, the main issue was that, by January, it looked a few weeks older than Christmas. To accommodate the filming, the management agreed to consolidate their merchandise — they remained open throughout the filming week — and allowed the crew to build Mount Olympus right in the heart of their main floor. Since the filming started after 6 p.m. on shooting days, many confused shoppers were privy to the spectacle of the large contraption made of wood, cotton batting, paper, and lots of sparkly, silver glitter. Those curious enough to ask were told a movie was being filmed, but many more likely just thought the department store was weeks late in dismantling their overly elaborate decorations for the holidays.

The children used as extras in the film were mostly the friends and family members of Higbee's employees. While the twelve-hour shoot certainly took a toll on the children, they weren't the only ones vulnerable to bouts of fatigue.

"I couldn't take off work, so I was pretty much working for twenty-four hours straight," Patty recalls. "After two days of doing that, I wasn't really acting my anger anymore. I hadn't slept in days. They put that suit and that heavy hat on me and I was ready to roll."

Each day, Patty would arrive at the store, get into her costume, have her makeup done, and be escorted to her makeshift dressing room in a conference room on the tenth floor. Long periods of waiting on a film set are the norm, and the department store location shoot was no different. Throughout the evening and well into the twilight hours, Patty would drift in and out of consciousness, often with a cup of coffee in one hand, waiting to be summoned on the walkie talkie by the production assistants.

"Being half dozy and dazed contributed greatly to my personification of evil," she jokes.

The one saving grace was that there were no more lost meals as a result of *A Christmas Story*. She may have had to skip lunch for her auditions, but she enjoyed full dinners in the middle of the night, courtesy of the film's producers.

"Usually on a set they'd round you up for a dinner call," she says. "They had us segregated. All the extras and everyone on the Santa line went somewhere else. They were getting things like macaroni and hamburger and we, the people with the contracts, were getting stuff like stuffed Cornish hens."

Being a professional actor may have had its perks, but it also had its drawbacks. The set was primarily made up of amateur and non-professional actors, with whom Patty and Drew Hocevar, her elfin partner-in-crime, had to act throughout most of the six-day shoot.

Drew initially tried to get cast in the film during a cattle call for extras to appear in the department store scenes. He was passed over, but ultimately earned the more substantial role of the male elf, Patty's assistant, when the casting director learned he had previously been hired at Higbee's to play a toy soldier and astronaut in their "Santaland" holiday experience.

While they appear to be of comparable importance on screen, there was a significant difference between the two actors. Patty signed a contract with

Drew Hocevar, Jeff Gillen, and Patty Johnson © MGM/UA Entertainment / Photofest

Patty Johnson and Peter Billingsley © MGM/UA Entertainment / Photofest

the film's producers and continues to collect residuals from the film to this day. Conversely, Drew requested a similar deal, but was told he'd be replaced if he demanded anything more than the hourly minimum wage for his acting services.

Despite their differences, they did have one thing in common — unending annoyance at having to endure dozens of takes because of the child extras they were working with.

"There were lots of moments in that movie that we had to do thirty, forty times, over and over again," she says. "Santa and the other elves just sat on their booties and watched from their little perches, but I had to go up and down those stairs, dragging those kids that were almost as big as me, up and down for every take. I'm picking 'em up off their feet and throwing 'em on Santa's lap, and I'm telling you, some of those kids shouldn't have been eating

Drew Hocevar and Jeff Gillen © MGM/UA Entertainment / Photofest

A CHRISTMAS STORY

carbs that year. It was not an easy job! That also helped me tremendously with my character. After your thirtieth or fortieth take of the same fifteen-second scene, it started to become something they call 'method acting.'"

According to Drew, Peter Billingsley was hardly ever responsible for any holdups. Unfortunately, the same can't be said for Ian Petrella. The young actor was afraid of the large set and would freak out whenever he made his way to the top of Mount Olympus.

"That kid got heavy after thirty times," Drew sighs, reflecting on the multitude of takes required to get the right shot.

However, that wasn't the only lack of focus Ian had on the set. Careful observers of the scene will notice moments of Randy breaking character and smiling off camera. Apparently, according to Petrella, the goof was all due to a girl named Celeste.

© MGM/UA Entertainment / Photofest

In the scene, several adult actors were dressed like characters from *The Wizard of Oz*. Celeste, who was standing behind Petrella in line, was deathly afraid of the Cowardly Lion and would break out into screams whenever the actor in feline clothing approached. Petrella found this hilarious, and even after she calmed down and stopped screaming, the memory of her cries ran through his head, occasionally making him giggle during the shooting of that scene.

While the kids were sometimes a source of irritation for the elves, they didn't seem to be a bother at all for director Bob Clark. As with the principal child actors, he seemed to have a unique ability to relate to the children and get the most out of their performances.

"The one thing I have found to be interesting, since I've been an adult, was the great job Bob Clark did with those kids," Patty says. "Oh my God, it was unbelievable. He just had those kids on task and they were having fun and he had everything going so smoothly. He was like a big kid himself, so he felt like he was part of the pack."

Not only was Clark fun for the children, but he also gave the adults on set plenty of reason to chuckle, too. Patty and Drew became fast friends and, during their downtime, they would visit Jeff Gillen, the actor inside the Santa suit, to share some laughs. The three would become filled with a little dash of worry and a big helping of holiday cheer whenever the director approached Mount Olympus, which was less unflinching than the nickname suggested.

"The set was not particularly stable," Patty says. "When people would come up and down those stairs, we would be trying to hang on for dear life up there. The worst-case scenario was when Bob Clark would run up those stairs and give us a direction. He liked to go down on that slide, so he'd plop himself down and we'd be airborne! And there was nothing to hold on to up

Bob Clark directs Peter Billingsley and Ian Petrella © MGM/UA Entertainment / Photofest

there. Once you were up near Santa's throne, you were screwed. There was nothing to hang on to. We had quite a few close calls up there."

At the bottom of the mountain, two special Higbee's customers stand out for careful observers of the film — writer Jean Shepherd turns up as the man in the black hat who tells Ralphie and Randy that the back of the line to see Santa is at the other end of the department store, along with his wife, Leigh Brown. While the sequence gets a lot of attention nowadays, when it was being filmed, Patty Johnson says Shepherd barely made an impression on her.

"I think I remember meeting him," she says. "But it wasn't a big thing. It was just sort of like, 'oh, here's the guy who wrote this.'"

Perhaps Shepherd chose this scene for his cameo appearance because it was one that had particular resonance for him. While the bulk of the movie is loosely based on his childhood experiences, the storyteller recalled in 1997 how this scene closely mirrored what occurred the first time he saw the jolly fat man in a department store.

Jeff Gillen and Peter Billingsley © MGM/UA Entertainment / Photofest

A CHRISTMAS STORY

"You know, I had been thinking for weeks what I wanted for Christmas," he said. "I figured the best thing to do was tell Santa Claus about that. I looked up at that Santa Claus and he had these big, watery blue eyes and a huge beard. He was so impressive that my mind went blank. It's like if all of a sudden you're sitting on the president's lap and he says, 'What would you like for me to pass in legislation, sonny?' Your mind's going to go blank!

"So, at that point, Santa Claus said, 'Ho-ho-ho, how 'bout a football, kid?' Football," he continued. "I wanted a BB gun! So he pushed me off his lap and this elf grabbed me and threw me down a slide that went down into the snow. I laid there for a minute and knew I wasn't a fit person to talk to the great Santa Claus [who was] obviously a star."

Filming wrapped after a Saturday daytime shoot. Patty returned the costume, thanked God that she would never have to wear that annoying headpiece ever again, and told the director she appreciated the opportunity.

On the seventh day she rested for the first time in almost a week.

CHAPTER THREE

St. Catharines and the No-Show Snow

The weeks following the Christmas holiday every year were always filled with excitement for the students of Victoria Public School in St. Catharines, Ontario. They would compare what Santa had brought each of them and which family members had given the most embarrassing gift. However, as it is the role of children to be distracted in the weeks immediately following an extended break from school, it is the role of the faculty to try to retain order and normalcy.

That is, of course, unless a production company asks to film a major

Bob Clark and
Ian Petrella
© Ian Petrella

motion picture in your school. If that happens, the faculty is allowed to throw formalities out the window. After all, the rules are meant to be broken. What better place is there to learn that valuable life lesson than in school?

Marshall Pomroy, the school principal in 1983, was faced with this very scenario and, as any reasonable administrator would, he seized the opportunity to promote his school and provide an excellent and, yes, educational experience to his students. "It sounds corny, but everyone's excited," he said at the time. "It will also give us an ideal opportunity to follow up after it's all over and try to incorporate some of the experiences into the school curriculum."

Although Cleveland has since been identified as the primary location for filming *A Christmas Story*, the majority of the movie was actually shot in Canada. Director Bob Clark made a second home of America's northern neighbor, and for many reasons, he preferred to shoot his movies there.

"I was recently in Cleveland and decided to go on the tour of the *Christmas Story* House," says Tyler Schwartz of RetroFestive, a company that sells replica leg lamps in Canada. "The guide said, 'The movie was shot in Cleveland and, oh, by the way, they popped up to Canada to shoot a couple scenes.' I understand why they tell that story, but it's not true at all.

"Bob Clark mostly made his movies in Canada, mostly for tax shelter purposes, but also because he had a place up here," Schwartz continues. "All his crew was Canadian. In many respects, it was a Canadian movie, and, oh, by the way, they popped *down* to Cleveland because that's where they found Higbee's and they needed a house nearby."

Because Clark's films were never big-budget productions, even after the amazing success of *Porky's*, he never had the luxury of sparing no expense when it came to filming. Canada provided an economic incentive for the filmmaker that enabled him to keep his costs low and his chance for strong returns high.

"He was always looking for a good deal and how to make his movies as affordably as he could," Schwartz continues. "Back in the day, Canada offered some of the best tax subsidies and that is the heart of why he shot his movies in Canada. I'm sure he appreciated Canadian actors, but it was cheaper to do it in Canada."

When it came time to search for the location that would serve as Warren G. Harding Elementary School, the director sent location manager Michael MacDonald and his team to Canada to find the perfect place that could appear to look like America in the 1940s. "We looked at a great number of cities, but this school and the surrounding neighborhood houses provided the period we needed," MacDonald said in 1983.

What set Victoria Public School apart from the others was not only the look and feel of the building but also how it would look on film in an establishing wide shot. The other schools under consideration had modern buildings behind them that would have been difficult to work around, so Victoria, framed by nothing but trees and sky, came out on top.

MacDonald approached the principal, presented him with a script, and asked for permission to not only shoot the film at Victoria Public School but also use the students as extras in the movie. The principal was receptive and, with the approval of the school board, a quick decision was made to move forward with the project.

Christmas Tree Films made an unusual offer to the school district for the ability to use their building and cast their students as extras. The school would be paid $3.50 per hour for each of the students working as extras. In essence, the kids would be donating their time to the school district.

"All the kids received a dollar," Tyler Schwartz says. "I used to think it was a dollar a day, but no, it was actually just a dollar, so they'd be on the books. I'm not sure if this would have happened in the United States in 1983, but it happened at St. Catharines."

Auditions were held on January 7 for schoolchildren to serve as extras. Michael MacDonald put all the students through a quick screen test and took their photographs. They were divided into two groups: twenty students who would serve as Ralphie's classmates in the classroom scenes, and those who would be the onlookers for the exterior shots near the flagpole. The students' parents were given contracts and invited to sign on the dotted line. Their kids were about to be in a major motion picture.

For the students, the thrill of being cast in a movie was exciting, even if they were barely receiving enough monetary compensation to purchase a candy bar between takes.

"I'm so excited, I've never been asked to be in a movie before," eleven-year-old Rhonda Seligy said as she was being fitted for a costume. "I want to work my way up to Hollywood, and my mom thinks I'm going to make it. She told me to smile and talk clearly."

Ernest Harris Jr., who was in fifth grade at the time, says he and his younger siblings, Julene and Vic, were selected as extras because they were the only black family at the school. The affirmative-action casting decision didn't get in the way of the delight he felt when he was told he'd been chosen to appear in the film. "It was completely amazing," he said. "I remember high-fiving a friend in the hall when we found out we'd be in the classroom scene. Someone else did a cartwheel. It was completely spectacular."

The only significant snag that came out of the screen test and costume fittings was that the boys had to get 1940s haircuts. Some of the boys only agreed reluctantly to allow the team from St. Catharines' Career School of Hairdressing to cut their hair in one of the classrooms, but others didn't mind, as long as they were going to be included in the movie: "I don't really care about that," eleven-year-old Jeff Nickerson said. "I'm just lucky to get the chance."

The students of Victoria Public School getting their hair cut © Anne Dean

For the role of the teacher, Miss Shields, director Bob Clark went to Tedde Moore, a veteran actress of the stage and screen, whom he first met when she auditioned for a role in his 1979 film *Murder by Decree*. "He just hired me to play Donald Sutherland's wife [in the film]," Moore explains. "I was four months pregnant, but off I went to England to make this movie and it was a success. It was one of my great lifetime experiences, and I always consider really good experiences in the theater or in film gifts because they don't happen very often. Most of the time acting feels like work, but I felt *Murder by Decree* was a great gift."

A year later, when the director was seeking an actress for his next film, Moore once again hoped to land a part. "I met Bob Clark again when I auditioned for his 1980 film *Tribute*," she recalls. "The call went out for an actor prepared to expose her breasts on screen. In those days it was a big issue and a lot of actors took great offense to being asked those things. So Bob being Bob said, 'Here's the deal,' before anyone came in. 'I don't want to have that discussion with them. They need to know that at some point in the script she rips her shirt off.' So, me being me, I'm a dreadful exhibitionist, I said 'I'm there.' I thought the script was wonderful and I knew Jack Lemmon was going to be in it and I thought, 'Wow! How fantastic,' [and] I went and auditioned for him, but I didn't get that role."

After her second audition for Clark, Moore appeared in the 1981 film *The Amateur* and continued taking bit parts on television. "Bob was editing *Porky's 2* when he ran into my husband, Don Shebib, who is a filmmaker and was good friends with him," Moore continues. "Bob said, 'Oh, I have a part for Tedde in my next film. Get her to call me, I'm shooting in minutes.'"

Although her husband knew Moore enjoyed working with Clark, Shebib believed there was an insurmountable obstacle that would keep his wife from the role. "Don said, 'Well, I'm afraid she won't be able to do it,'" Moore explains. "At that point I was about seven months pregnant. From what I understand there was a lot of 'guy talk' about why I was always pregnant. Even so, Bob said, 'Well, we'll meet anyway.'

"So I went over to meet Bob, and I was really showing a lot," she continues. "As you know, the film took place in the late 1930s/early 1940s, and in those days not only were pregnant women unable to teach, but until the war began, married women didn't teach because it was deemed inappropriate that they stood up in front of children, for fear the kids would be thinking about their teacher fucking. I mean, can you believe the way people thought in those days? So there was no way I was going to be able to play this role as a pregnant person. So Bob said, 'Don't worry, we'll sort it. I'll put you behind a desk. I want you to be in this part.' It was extremely flattering."

Moore accepted the part of Miss Shields, but once she got back home, she developed cold feet. Did she really want to be sixty pounds overweight and permanently seated behind a desk in her first MGM film? There was no way in hell. She knew she needed to come up with a solution, and fast. As she was thinking of a way to solve her problem, her mind wandered to a childhood memory that ended up providing inspiration.

"I started thinking about my most-loathed teacher, Miss Parker, the woman I had when I was in grade three," she recalls. "The shape of Miss Parker was the shape of the queen mother, which was this strange oneness. Because of the undergarments in those days, women's boobies never stayed up. They kind of drooped down to their tummies, which were kind of big because they had these babies and nobody knew about exercise, so they had this shape that was all one fatness."

Moore knew she had found the solution. "I called Bob and I said, 'There was a very, very typical look for women in the 1930s. I think we can achieve that with padding,' and he flipped. He was so happy. He thought this was the greatest idea."

With Moore's scenes scheduled to shoot weeks after she was cast, production went into overdrive to round out her figure. Clark hired a theatrical costumer to design and construct the padding. By the time Moore's scenes were shot, she was eight months pregnant, but it's virtually unnoticeable in the film. "If you really examine it, there's one moment when I'm talking to Flick and you can see how taut the fatness is in the front of my stomach, which is not what fat people are," she admits. "They're soft, they aren't hard. You can just see it for one moment if you're really looking for it."

While most involved with *A Christmas Story* tried to keep Moore's pregnancy under wraps in the film, at least one person is proud to explain the actress's fuller figure in the film: Noah Shebib, whom music lovers may know by his stage name, "40," but whom Moore simply knows as "my son." Due to her pregnancy, the holiday film could be considered 40's first professional credit. "She's got a big belly [in the movie] because it's me," 40 says. "I'm in that film."

The fact that the illusion went off without a hitch isn't to say that Moore's stuffing didn't have bizarre side effects. "The funny part was, when I would go home at night after shooting all day, I would dream that I actually wasn't pregnant," she says. "That it was all in my mind. It was very funny."

On January 28, the circus from Hollywood arrived at Victoria Public School. Trucks arrived with furniture, lights, and wardrobe. Outside, monkey bars were erected and the Canadian flag was taken off the pole in exchange for the stars and stripes. Neighbors were asked to move their cars from the block and classic cars from the late 1930s were put in their place. The school basement was converted into a makeup room, while

One of the makeshift dressing rooms in the school
© Anne Dean

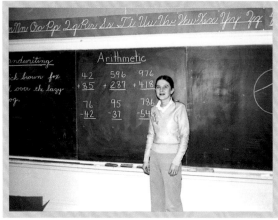

Victoria School teacher
Anne Dean poses next
to the chalkboard she
wrote on for filming
© Anne Dean

an upstairs classroom became the fitting room for costumes.

Shooting began as scheduled on Monday, January 31. The students who were serving as extras were given a 7 a.m. call for hair, makeup, and costuming. Hours before that, trailers and equipment swarmed the school parking lot. A science classroom was emptied out and vintage wooden desks were brought in to take the school back in time by four decades.

The first scene filmed was of the school-children saying, "Good morning, Miss Shields!" with their mouths full of false teeth. The kids got a crash course in filmmaking 101 — often it's a lot of hurry up and wait.

"It took forever and [the teeth] were uncomfortable and tasted horrible," Mary Jo Schmidt, who was in third grade at the time of filming, recalls. "I still dread seeing any of those false teeth things."

Although twenty students had been delegated as Ralphie's classmates, four students had to be transferred to the more general exterior shots because the filmmakers found themselves short on vintage desks. There were a few tears among the children when they realized they had to return to their regularly scheduled classes, but the shoot pressed on.

The interior shots of Victoria Public School went off excellently, but once it was time to film the playground sequences around the flagpole, the filmmakers found themselves unable to continue because of a lack of snow.

"The weather did not cooperate," Victoria Public School teacher Anne Dean recalled in an April 1983 account to the Lincoln County Board of Education. "Once the indoor scenes were shot, everything was packed up and off they went to the studio in Toronto."

This isn't to say that the filmmakers hadn't resorted to artificial snow before when the weather hadn't cooperated. After shooting the Higbee's sequences in Cleveland, Bob Clark and his team shot for an additional week in the town. During this time, the crew worked on what was arguably their most ambitious sequence of the film — an outdoor parade that opens the movie in the Cleveland town square.

"We all had a blast working there because this was just post-Christmas," Peter Billingsley remembers. "They had kept the downtown square in all that flavor for us. We were shooting lengthy, lengthy nights, so we as kids were sleeping all day and then up all night, which I'm sure was a handful for Bob."

According to the film's production notes, 6,000 feet of emerald-colored garlands and 75,000 watts of twinkling Christmas lights were hung throughout the square. The modern bus shelters were covered with a façade to make them look like they were from the Depression era, and dozens of antique vehicles were loaned to Christmas Tree Films from local residents to help complete the 1940s feel.

The Parker family in the town square © MGM/UA Entertainment / Photofest

A number of real-life Clevelanders were asked to participate, including the Holy Trinity Baptist Church Ensemble, the Revere High School Band, the Ohio Boys Choir, and the North East Ohio Salvation Army Band. The inclusion of these groups helped make the parade enjoyable for all the participants, which thus created an authentic scene. In many aspects, the celebration really did take on a life of its own, which Bob Clark was lucky enough to capture on film.

"The [Holy Trinity Baptist Church Ensemble] was just hired as extras," says Carl Zittrer, one of the film's composers who was present during the parade. "They started singing 'Go Tell It on the Mountain' on the street just because it was cold. I saw them and said, 'Oh my God, this is gold.' They weren't hired to sing, they were just hired to be there. They didn't want to be paid, but we donated money to their church.

"Well, I heard them doing this, I said, 'We can't not record this,'" he continues. "That was really my decision, because Bob didn't know where they were. The set was pandemonium. He was half a block away from them. He probably forgot they were there. I said, 'Hey! Bob! Come over here!' and then he just fell in love with their singing. I think it lasts about ten seconds in the finished movie, but it really enriches the tapestry of that scene."

In Cleveland, the filmmakers were treated to everything they wanted, except for snow. The winter of 1982 was the warmest winter in the state's recorded history, which was probably fantastic for the locals, but it was definitely horrible for the imported cast and crew attempting to film a Christmas movie. There was a light snowstorm the night before the parade scene was filmed, which provided a dusting on the ground during those shots, but help was needed.

Special effects supervisor Martin Malivoire and his assistant Neil Trifunovich devoted their time in the early days of the Cleveland shoot to tracking down snow from every corner of the United States. Initially, it was thought that snow would be imported from Northern Michigan or Buffalo, New York, but it proved to be cost- and time-prohibitive. Ultimately, snow arrived with the assistance of potato flakes, which were blown about by large wind machines; large bales of shredded vinyl, which were used on set pieces to make it appear like snow had fallen and stuck; and firefighters' foam, which was sprayed on the grass and sidewalks to give the impression that heavy snowfall had occurred the night before. For the Cleveland scenes, artificial snow could be brought in because it was needed only to cover specific sections of the landscape. It was possible to only cover one section of cement and a few trees with artificial snow, while the rest of the block remained untouched. This saved not only on cost but also on the time that would be spent laying the artificial dusting.

Bob Clark liked to tell of a passerby who was driving through the neighborhood where they were shooting outside the Parker house, whose face registered a look of complete bewilderment at the sight of a snow-covered street. "All of a sudden, he rounds a corner, one he sees every day, and one half of the street is covered with snow — houses, trees, everything. He looked like he thought he'd just entered the Twilight Zone!"

With the snow situation mastered in Cleveland, one might have thought that the lack of snow would be a non-issue at Victoria Public School, where they had to shoot the now-infamous flagpole sequence in which Ralphie's pal Flick is "triple-dog-dared" to put his tongue to a freezing metal pole. But fabricated snow was impossible for the schoolyard shoot. To make it look realistic, snow would have to cover the entire field. This would have been difficult, expensive, and time-consuming. On top of that, the weather was too warm for artificial snow to hold up. While the interior classroom shots were being filmed, the production team closely watched the weather report. The goal was to remain at Victoria Public School through February 6, but the crew made the decision to leave three days early due to the lack of inclement weather. The students were told they wouldn't be needed for shooting and that they'd be having their regularly scheduled classes for the remainder of the week.

"The weather certainly isn't giving us a break," location manager Michael MacDonald said at the time. "We'll be going back to Toronto to shoot indoors. But we'll be back here at the first opportunity."

On February 3, everything was packed up. The school hallways, which had been filled with furniture and lights, were cleared out. The science classroom that had become Miss Shields' temporary domain was restored to its prior state. All students returned to their classes, nearly a hundred of them uncertain as to whether or not they'd actually end up being included in the movie, or if Christmas Tree Films would find another location with more exciting weather.

As fate would have it, on February 6, just as the crew was originally scheduled to pack up and go home, a delayed Christmas miracle occurred — it snowed. Even though it was a Sunday, all the schoolchildren reported at 7:30 a.m. for the outdoor shoot. The crews were ready and rolling and, in the extremely cold temperatures, the young Scott Schwartz prepared for his big scene.

The fourteen-year-old pint-size actor had made his film debut in *The Toy* (1982), in which he received third-billing behind Hollywood heavyweights Richard Pryor and Jackie Gleason. Although the movie was panned by critics, it was a box office success, which led to the young actor receiving a leading role in *Kidco*, which was shot in 1982 but released two years later.

Before he had an opportunity to bask in the glow of having completed his second film, Schwartz received an invitation that would lead to the definitive work of his film career. "I had just finished up shooting *Kidco* and Bob Clark had just seen *The Toy*," Schwartz recalls. "He wanted to meet me for one of the kids. He wasn't even sure which character until we met and talked."

Like the majority of the rest of the cast, Schwartz's audition for Clark was unconventional. "My audition was just an hour conversation, then lunch," he says. "Before I had even got home, I had the job."

While Schwartz knew he was cast in the film, he was unaware as to exactly what his new job entailed. "When I got the movie, believe it or not,

I thought I was playing Ralphie," he admits. "I had been the lead in *The Toy* and I had been the lead in *Kidco*, so I figured I was the lead in *A Christmas Story*."

The actor's delusions of grandeur were upheld until the day of the first table read with the rest of the cast. "They sent me the script, didn't say anything, and I was memorizing Ralphie's lines," he explains. "We get up to reading the script and Bob Clark goes, 'Okay, Zack, you're going to play Scut Farkus, and Yano, you're going to be Grover Dill, Scott, you're going to be Flick, and R.D., you're going to be Schwartz.' I turned around — my father was sitting behind me — and I go 'Flick? Huh?!' And Bob goes, 'You know, Peter, you're going to be Ralphie.'"

Although he was civil during the table read, Schwartz remained silently perturbed about his situation. "*A mistake must have been made,*" he thought. "*Does Bob Clark realize that I just starred in two movies with big Hollywood icons?*"

Scott Schwartz, Peter Billingsley, and R.D. Robb © St. Catharines Museum

The experience of working with show business royalty so early on in his career gave Schwartz the confidence to discuss the problem with Clark, despite his young age and small stature.

"Bob, are you sure about this?" Schwartz said. "You know, I've been the lead in . . ."

"No, no, you're Flick. That's your role, you'll be fine," Clark replied. "I know it's not a big role, but it's not the size of the role, it's what you make out of it, and I think you're going to do a great job."

With that, Schwartz made peace with his role and Flick was born. Not only did he make the most out of his time on screen, but he also had a lot of fun behind the scenes. He and Peter Billingsley got along famously and often would terrorize the adult members of the cast and crew.

"We were stuck in a hotel, so we had to entertain ourselves," Schwartz explains. However, despite his best efforts to make Billingsley guilty by association, his *Christmas Story* peers mutually agree that Schwartz was the catalyst for many of the shenanigans that would generally land a kid on Santa's naughty list.

"Scott was definitely the leader of us all," clarifies R.D. Robb, who played Schwartz, the kid who initiated the triple-dog-dare. "He was the oldest and talked a big game. He was the most experienced in every way and got us into some trouble."

While Scott might have been the brainchild for a lot of pranks, Peter was often close behind: "I remember Peter throwing water balloons off the fourteenth-story balcony of his hotel room," recalls Zack Ward, who played neighborhood bully Scut Farkus. The kids would often run around the hotel, banging on doors, pretending to be members of the housekeeping staff. On one occasion, Schwartz ordered several hundred dollars' worth of pizza for Darren McGavin. The young cast members would have hated to deny anyone the opportunity to be included in the fun, so McGavin wasn't the only person to get a surprise cart of food in the middle of the night. "I think Bob also got some unwanted room service," Schwartz says with a laugh, still amused by his childhood antics.

In addition to the fun the kids had in the hotel, they also managed to have an enjoyable time while shooting. When it came time to film Flick's unforgettable tongue-touch with a metal flagpole, the kids couldn't wait to test out the special effect. "Of course we all had to try it," Peter Billingsley says. "It was so cool."

According to Schwartz, there was a small generator motor buried in sand with a tube sticking out of it. The tube ran through a long, cylindrical piece of plastic that went over a real flagpole and was painted to look like rusted metal. The mechanism acted like a vacuum and had a tiny hole where the actor would place his tongue to make it appear as if he was frozen on the flagpole.

The crew testing the flagpole mechanism © Anne Dean

Although Billingsley remembers all the kids testing out the effect, Schwartz remembers seeing only one other person put his tongue to the jerry-rigged flagpole. "Bob did it to show me it wasn't going to hurt," Schwartz explains. "The pole was painted and my tongue would wipe the paint away, so they'd have to touch it up whenever I put my tongue to it."

Shooting the short scene took twelve hours over two days. The conditions were freezing and the cast and crew had to brainstorm ways to stay comfortable in the extreme temperature.

"All afternoon we were frozen," recalls teacher Anne Dean. "The children didn't want to 'play' anymore. It was miserable."

"It was twenty-five degrees below zero with the windchill," Schwartz says. To adjust to the extreme temperature, the actor used over sixty hand warmers during the day and wore electric socks with large C-batteries pressed against his ankles. When not filming, the filmmakers came up with a plan to keep the kids warm during their downtime, but the results were unsuccessful.

"They had a car for us to sit in between takes," says Schwartz, "but it was too noisy when they were shooting, so they'd cut it off while filming. Then they'd yell, 'Cut!' and we'd run back to the car and all the heat would be gone. It would be freezing."

For the kids, there was another unexpected side effect of the outdoor shoot at Victoria Public School. Several dozen students who weren't cast as extras were showing up at the field and asking the actors for their signatures.

"It was just so bitter cold," Schwartz recalls. "My hands were blue and people wanted for me to stick around and sign autographs. It was crazy."

The craziness continued when Schwartz, who quickly earned a reputation as being a brat on the set, got his comeuppance for all of the pranks he pulled on the cast and crew during the shoot. "Scott was a pain in the ass," R.D. Robb explains. "The crew was screwing around with him one time and, when we broke for lunch, everyone walked away and left him stuck on the flagpole."

R.D. Robb retreating into his trailer to escape the cold © Anne Dean

"I was out there all by myself," Schwartz remembers. "There was no one out there!" In a true moment of life imitating art, the cast and crew watched from a distance as Scott Schwartz became Flick. "He was literally failing his arms, just like in the movie," Robb says, laughing. "He was yelling, 'Hey guys, come back! Come back!' It was so funny."

One of the prominently featured students in the film, a redheaded boy who yells, "Holy cow, it's the fire department!" and "Wow, it's the cops!" was actually not one of the children selected from the school. Tom Wallace earned his role as one of the only non-principal actors with speaking lines in that scene because he lived in the rural community of Campbellford in Eastern Ontario, right next door to a cottage owned by Bob Clark and his wife.

Since the Clarks weren't always there, they had hired the thirteen-year-old Wallace to maintain their yard. One day, the filmmaker saw Wallace cutting the grass and approached him. "Hey," he said. "Wanna be in a movie?"

The details were ironed out with the Wallace parents. Clark said he was filming what would be "a Christmas classic," and their youngster made his way to St. Catharines to be one of many schoolchildren in the movie. He was treated to the same 1940s haircut, which he enjoyed getting just about as much as the boys at Victoria Public School had. Initially, he had no lines, but as filming progressed, Clark found a way to feature his neighbor more prominently in the picture.

For Wallace, filming was a lot of fun. He recalls playing hockey during his downtime and receiving a comparably hefty fee of $500 for his services, a substantial amount more than the single dollar the Victoria students were paid.

When the film was completed, his local movie theater promoted the fact that he was in *A Christmas Story*. An advertising campaign featured Wallace as a local celebrity, even if it was only for a few short weeks.

Once Flick's tongue was severed from the pole with the assistance of Neil Burton and John Kennedy, two locals who acted as firefighters, it was believed the shooting was done. The trailers left the parking lot, the rented wind machines were returned, and the actors made their way back to Toronto.

With the ice-cold shooting conditions and the occasional inconveniences beyond the camera's gaze, Schwartz was happy when filming wrapped on that scene at the end of a long day. That was, until director Bob Clark approached him a few days later.

The view of filming from inside the school
© Anne Dean

The Victoria School students warming themselves between takes © Anne Dean

"Bob came up to me and said, 'Listen, we have some good news and some bad news,'" Schwartz recalls. "The good news is you're gonna be with us for an extra few days. The bad news is it's because when we shot the film, they underdeveloped it in processing. We're going to have to reshoot it."

The underdeveloped film would have caused the scene to look significantly lighter than the rest of the movie. As a result, Clark scheduled a day for Schwartz and the kids to venture back to the same shooting location to recreate the magic they had captured on their first time filming the scene. There were no problems in processing the second time around, and the reshot scene is the version that appears in the film.

The reshoots included a scene shot by the jungle gym in the playground, and on February 10 and 11, they finished the last shots of the Victoria Public School filming. Once again, the bitter cold was an issue, cutting through the ratty costumes the child actors and extras were required to wear.

To help supplement what the costumers provided, the producers asked the parents of the Victoria Public School children to search for any old clothes that might be appropriate for the students to wear during the shoot. Cory Ireland, who was in fourth grade at the time, remembers wearing an old plaid wool jacket his mother found for him: "It was a big mistake. We were filming the pole scene and it was freezing."

(Above) Peter Billingsley playing with Legos between takes (Below) Scott Schwartz (right) joking around with one of the Victoria School students © Anne Dean

This isn't to say it was all work and no play. The actors seemed to enjoy their time at the school, and often spent their downtime playing hockey or soccer in the gym. According to Ireland, the child actors also had a habit of taking Play-Doh and chucking it at the school walls. "They were allowed to do what they wanted," he says, "and we kind of tagged along for fun."

The kids at the school were certainly taken with their brush with Hollywood, and the film's actors and crew reciprocated the warm feelings.

"The kids [from the school] were remarkably good," Bob Clark reflected in 2003. Tedde Moore agrees. "The kids in the classroom were wonderful," she says. "We all had a good time. Kids love acting. It's easy for them to do."

For all of the professionalism the kids showed while filming, Moore does remember one memorable encounter with the young Scott Schwartz before filming got underway for the flagpole scene, which showed the unpredictability of dealing with child actors. "Scotty got in the makeup chair before I did, and he was as much of a character then as he is now," she says. "I liked him very much, but he freaked me out. One day I said to the darling makeup man who had been there for a long time that I was never, never, ever going to let any of my children be a screen actor. This was all because Scotty had just been in the chair and had been talking about how much he loved reading *Playboy*. The makeup artist was putting makeup on my face and said, 'How old do you think Scott is?' I told him I didn't know and guessed eleven or twelve. It turned out that he was like fifteen or something. He was one of those young adults that work in Hollywood that were smaller and looked younger.

"It was hilarious," she continues with a laugh. "I had no idea the lad was actually as old as he was. It was pretty funny. I was just horrified that this young boy was behaving like this teenager, but it turns out he had every right to behave like that because he was one."

When *A Christmas Story* was finished, Bob Clark wanted to do something nice for the young extras who had endured the extreme changes to their school schedule for a few weeks, often in the freezing cold while filming take after take of the same crowd shots. The studio treated them to a screening of the film at Lincoln Mall Cinema, a movie theater nearby. The entire school went on the field trip and, when they first saw the establishing shot of the fictional Warren G. Harding Elementary School, they erupted into thunderous applause and loud howling.

When the movie was over, the kids gave the film rave reviews. "I loved it," twelve-year-old Kenny Vallee said. "I'm gonna see it a few more times. It's just great because nothing like this ever happened here before."

The principal was also pleased with the finished product. "I thought the kids did very well," Marshall Pomroy said. "They were quite photogenic. It was interesting to see them."

However, not everyone was pleased with the film. The *St. Catharines Standard*, the local newspaper in the town, cited one of the teachers at the school as being disappointed that the film wasn't a "real wholesome movie." While she had no complaints with the way the students of Victoria Public School were represented in the film, Ivy Hunt took umbrage at the scenes in which Ralphie gets out of bad situations by lying, such as when his mother catches him cursing and he claims to have learned the bad words from his pal Schwartz. One such scene was filmed in the school: Ralphie denies knowing who triple-dog-dared Flick to put his tongue to the flagpole. According to the *Standard*, Hunt's main concern was that lying was celebrated and used for comic effect.

However, Hunt seemed to represent a minority opinion. The school community embraced the film and it remains a much talked about event in St. Catharines to this day.

Bob Clark donated one final gift to the school — a care package containing a movie poster, a copy of the script signed by "their teacher" Tedde Moore and "classmate" Peter Billingsley, and a Betamax tape labeled "*A Christmas Story — Director's Cut.*" When the principal and students buried those objects in a time capsule in the front yard of the school, they had no idea that decades later the videotape would be one of the most sought-after artifacts from the film.

CHAPTER FOUR

Indiana,
Canada

Eight-year-old Ian Petrella sat at the dinner table across from Darren McGavin, who was reading his newspaper. To his left sat Melinda Dillon, with large blond hair that made her look a little bit like a sparkler on the Fourth of July. Peter Billingsley sat across from her, buttering a thick slice of bread. Ian, who was wearing a pink bib and a maroon sweater, lifted his dinner plate and planted his face in his food. The youngster put the plate back down, laughing like a demented clown, as meatloaf and mashed potatoes stuck to his nose and chin.

Ian Petrella getting ready for his snowsuit scene
© Ian Petrella

Peter Billingsley and Ian Petrella © Ian Petrella

It was one of the many shooting days spent at Madger Studios in Toronto. On this day, the "Mommy's Little Piggy" sequence, as fans of the film have come to call it, was being shot. For the young Ian, filming the scene was a real test of endurance. "It was something you had to do over and over because this was the time when you only had one 35mm camera to shoot a movie with," Petrella says. "If you needed different angles, you'd have to break that camera down. It was about an hour between takes."

To make the young actor laugh, director Bob Clark would hide on the set with Ian's mother, the two cracking jokes and making farting noises from their mouths. What came out was genuine elation and a memorable laugh. The sound of his giggle has stuck with fans of the film, and consequently has become unshakable to the now-adult Ian.

"People will come up to me and they'll ask me to do the laugh or recite a line from the film," he says. "I always tell them I can't. First of all, I'm in my thirties and it's just not going to sound the same. Some people get kind of pissed about it, like 'Why can't you do it? Why won't you do it?' and I tell them, 'Because it's not going to sound the same! That's just how it is.'"

Clark seemed to have a very simple rule when it came to directing kid actors: if they think it's funny, it probably is. As a result, all the young actors were encouraged to experiment on the set and make suggestions to help enhance a scene. "There was a lot of play that we got to do," Ian says. "It wasn't really acting. We didn't have to think too much; we just did it and had a lot of fun."

Tedde Moore also had an enjoyable time during the Toronto shoot. Though her scenes in the film were shot in St. Catharines, the actress did have a scene on the soundstage several weeks after her initial *Christmas Story* stint wrapped. Moore appeared alongside Melinda Dillon and Darren McGavin in a sequence that was cut before the movie's theatrical release. The original shooting script indicates that after Ralphie writes his theme about how much he wants a Red Ryder BB gun for Christmas, a fantasy sequence follows. Miss Shields makes her way to the Parker house to sing Ralphie's praises and help make the case for him to get his desired Christmas gift. Before she leaves, she gives the parents clear instructions: "If you have any questions about what I have just said, please write them in a theme of 100 words or less for Ralph to deliver to me at school," she said. "I will grade it and return it by next Friday."

Even though the scene didn't survive in the finished film, traces of it did remain in another one of Ralphie's dream sequences. "There's that scene where I'm dressed in a hat and an old-fashioned dress and I'm going 'A+, A+, A+,' which apparently comes out of nowhere," Moore says. "Why am I dressed this way? That's the way Ralphie saw me in his fantasies — a ginormous, imposing woman. I dressed in the same costume in the cut scene where I went to his house."

Darren McGavin
© Ian Petrella

Even though she has no cinematic record of the experience, she still regards working with Darren McGavin as one of the best experiences making the movie. "He rarely had a chance to play a theatrical scene in his movie life, so we just had a ball," she says fondly.

A number of other scenes were also cut from *A Christmas Story* before it was released. Reportedly, the "director's cut" version of the film clocked in at close to two hours. MGM argued that it should be shortened by a half hour, in order to have more screenings in movie theaters. While an alternate opening sequence was also cut (it was an extended version of Jean Shepherd's narration over establishing shots of steel mills), the bulk of the scenes that were cut

Dwayne McLean (center) as Black Bart with his young bandits © Ian Petrella

were Ralphie's fantasy sequences. From a practical standpoint, cutting those scenes could be done with minimal impact to the plot. For example, a sequence in which Ralphie rescues Santa Claus on the roof of a fairytale home was removed near the end of the film. The jolly gift-giver is about to be robbed by Black Bart and his band of brigands, but they prove to be no match for the tyke with a toy rifle.

The most significant cut to the movie was an elaborate big-budget sequence in which Ralphie frees Flash Gordon from the stronghold of Ming the Merciless. Careful observers of the movie may have noticed that the end credits reference this scene even though it doesn't appear in the finished version of the film.

"A good chunk of the budget went into that thing 'cause it was a huge set that they had built," Peter Billingsley says. "They had me in a little silver bikini and I was palling up with a space hero, taking on a big alien with a gun."

Billingsley may have been happy that the world didn't get to see him in his silver getup, but one person was unhappy about the decision to cut the elaborate sequence — Paul Hubbard, the actor who played Flash Gordon. "I read for it a few times," he says. "It was just an amazing set, very extensive. Mr. Clark spared no expense. I was thrilled when I saw the version with all our scenes intact. I was over the moon, and I was flabbergasted when I was told that a number of scenes were taken out. I never found out what the reason was."

Not only did he not know the reason, but he didn't find out his scene was taken out of the movie until a few weeks before Christmas, after the movie was already released in theaters. "My brother went to go see it and told me," he says. "I had young kids at the time and we were working on the nursery, so it took me a little while before I could see it for myself."

Peter Billingsley and Paul Hubbard in the deleted Flash Gordon scene © MGM/UA Entertainment / Photofest

Even though he wasn't in the movie, his name still appears in the end credits. According to Hubbard, that was an act of generosity on the part of Christmas Tree Films, which enabled the actor to continue to receive royalty checks for his performance, even though it was cut. Three decades later, *A Christmas Story* remains a high point of his career, even though few have seen his work on the project. "It was a blast doing it," he said. "I worked with great people and it was a great shoot. I was very proud to have been involved."

While MGM is most frequently blamed for the cuts to the film, director Bob Clark maintains that the final decision to take scenes out of the movie was his. "I cut [them] out," he said in 2003. "I had complete control of the film. In the first running of the film [they] should have been cut. We were storied out and we were ready to get on with our adventure."

Even if the film was stronger due to the cuts, many held out hope that one of the DVD releases of the movie would include the previously unseen footage. Tedde Moore was among those disappointed when she learned the deleted scenes would most likely never see the light of day.

"I was so delighted when I heard they were releasing the special edition of the DVD," she recalls. "I assumed my scene with Darren McGavin would be included. I phoned Bob and was heartbroken."

"We don't have it," Clark said.

"What do you mean?"

"The footage. We didn't save it. It doesn't exist."

And with that, nearly twenty minutes of one of the most popular holiday films of all time became reduced to nothing more than a memory for a select few.

The shots outside of the Parker home were filmed in Cleveland, but all of the interior shots were completed on the Toronto soundstage. In some cases, like during the filming of the leg lamp scene, this had the potential of causing a continuity nightmare for the actors since some brief sequences were shot in two different countries weeks apart. For example, the scene in which the Old Man is standing on the street along with his curious neighbor Swede, played with a Southern accent by Bob Clark in a Hitchcockian cameo, was filmed over a month after the interior shots. This sequence, which ranks as the favorite of Peter Billingsley and millions of *Christmas Story* fans worldwide, is memorable because of the sexy fishnet-covered porcelain leg that the Old Man receives as his major award. Reuben Freed, the production designer on the film, submitted sketches to Jean Shepherd until the writer settled on one that was agreeable to him.

The Bumpus hounds and their handlers © Ian Petrella

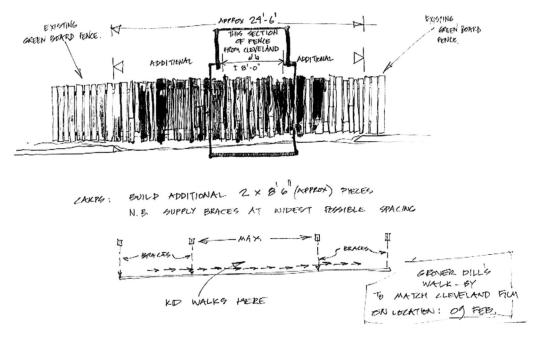

Reuben Freed's sketch for the alleyway scene. Notice a piece was brought to Canada from Cleveland for continuity. © Reuben Freed

While designing the leg, the production designer started with the description in Shepherd's original short story "My Old Man and the Lascivious Special Award That Heralded the Birth of Pop Art." The leg was described as being similar to the type used in Nehi — pronounced "knee-high," get it?

— soda company advertisements during the 1920s. Freed was also able to glean some inspiration from the 1976 *Phantom of the Open Hearth* PBS special, which marked the first time Shep's short story was adapted for the screen, as well as the first appearance of the iconic lamp.

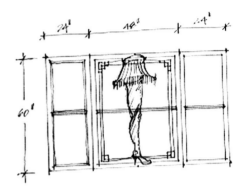

The main holdup in designing the lamp was what type of lampshade the appendage would wear. Several different styles were designed for Shepherd's approval, but the winning sketch was one that was reminiscent of an actual lamp Freed had in his childhood home. "I immediately thought of something I had seen in my mother's front room, which was sort of a gold-colored silk lampshade, pleated with fringe all around it," he says.

In total, three legs were made for production. Finding an original leg lamp has been considered the holy grail for *Christmas Story* fans, but the likelihood of finding one is about as great as locating Pee-wee Herman's bicycle in the basement of the Alamo. According to those involved in the production, all the lamps were destroyed during filming and none exist to this day.

While filming on the soundstage was relatively smooth sailing, one major distraction frequently got in the way of production — Jean Shepherd. The writer was often on the set while filming was underway, but instead of being a silent observer, he would pull the actors aside and give them direction. Director Bob Clark considered this a massive interference, and the two would often get into squabbles on the set.

"Listen, Pete," Shepherd would say, before making a beeline over to Peter Billingsley and giving him some suggestions to improve his performance. Clark would come running over as Shepherd walked away: "What did he just tell you?" The kid would reiterate the contradictory notes he'd just received to his director, who would immediately become incensed. He'd make his way over to Shepherd, who would casually be thumbing through his script on the other side of the room. "Jean, we can't *do* that, we just set this up!"

"Jean drove Bob Clark nuts," says Scott Schwartz. "It was hysterical.

Reuben Freed's original leg lamp design © Reuben Freed

(Above) Filming the soap poisoning scene © Ian Petrella
(Below) Jean Shepherd, c. 1972 © Photofest

There was never any specific heated argument or anything like that. It was just fun, wacky shit where Bob would have to go, 'Listen, Jean, do me a favor, will ya? You can't tell him something in the middle of the scene.'"

Ultimately, Clark had to ask Shepherd to stop coming to the set so they could remain on schedule. The young actors were fairly oblivious to the growing extent of their annoyance with each other, but looking back, they understand that Shepherd meant well.

"They were both so invested," Peter Billingsley says. "[They] had been with this a long time and had worked so hard."

"This is his life. This is his story," Ian Petrella says. "I'm sure he probably had a lot to say and he contributed as much as he could."

While the interior shots were being completed at Madger Studios, several exterior shots were being done throughout Toronto. Shepherd was still on the set when the fight between Ralphie and Scut Farkus was shot, and the writer once again had some very specific feedback for the young star.

"When I beat up the bully, [Jean] specifically wrote out [what I was supposed to say phonetically]," Billingsley says. "I still remember the beginning. There are some things from this movie that won't get out of my head. He wrote me three cards and told me to memorize it. He told me not to just try and get through it."

The young actor may have been able to get away with using faux-profanity during that scene, but when it came time to shoot the big "Oh, fudge!" sequence by the Cherry Street Bridge in Toronto on Valentine's Day, 1983, the

Ian Petrella
and Peter
Billingsley
© Ian Petrella

young actor got a chance to say "the queen mother of dirty words — the f-dash-dash-dash word." According to Billingsley, they filmed the sequence with him saying both versions of the profane word. The censored version was used for the audio, while the explicit version was used for the video to give the impression that Ralphie was really going to say it.

Filming wrapped on March 18. With a holiday deadline looming, Clark and his editor Stan Cole got to work. Carl Zittrer and Paul Zaza started on the score, which incorporated a mix of holiday tunes from period artists like Bing Crosby and the Andrews Sisters, classical music from composers like Prokofiev and Tchaikovsky, and original music cues. The rest of the cast and crew considered the project a part of their past and assumed that, as with most projects, it would be another footnote in their careers. If someone had told them that they would still be talking about *A Christmas Story* three decades later, none of them would have believed it.

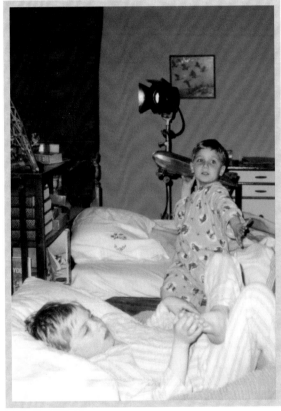

Peter Billingsley and Ian Petrella © Ian Petrella

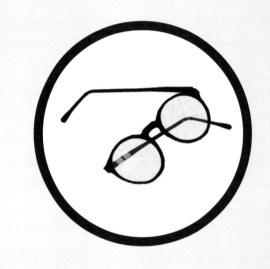

CHAPTER FIVE

Reconstructing
Christmas

A *Christmas Story* was a modest hit in 1983 when it debuted in theaters, but it was far from a runaway success. "The film was not just ignored. It was disliked by MGM," Tedde Moore says. "They thought it was crapola. They didn't even want to release it."

For director Bob Clark, *A Christmas Story*'s limited box office returns were the direct result of the studio's negligent attitude toward promotion and release of the project. "I was disappointed [by the film's financial intake] only because we had a hit," Clark said in 2003. "We had three weekends [in

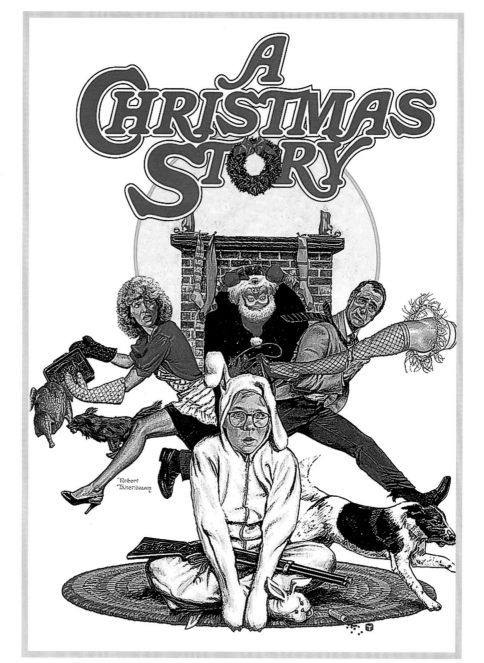

the] Christmas [season] that year. Sometimes you have two. We would have done $6, 7, 8 million dollars in each one. It grossed $18 million at the box office and we would have ended up doing $45 [million] or something like that which, in 1983, would have been a hugely successful movie, especially for a movie that cost $4 million."

However, the film didn't run for all three weekends of the Christmas season. In fact, it barely ran during Christmas at all. *A Christmas Story* was released on November 18, 1983, where it debuted as the #3 movie of the weekend with just over $2 million earned over 886 screens. In the following weekend, over the Thanksgiving holiday, the film expanded its presence to 938 screens and actually moved into the #1 slot with $3.9 million. However, the film quickly lost steam at cineplexes and by Christmas was playing in only a handful of theaters.

While Clark's estimates that the film would have grossed $45 million seem hyper-optimistic, one can't ignore the power the film had over Thanksgiving weekend and wonder how history might have been different if the movie had actually had the opportunity to play during the time when it presumably would have done the most business of the year.

And while Clark, and arguably some of the actors as well, has blamed the studio for the film's initial modest box office returns, Moore disagrees with that analysis: "I don't think [the film's initial box office] was necessarily the fault of MGM," she says. "There are endless stories about actors who turn down movies because they thought they were awful and [then they] turned out to be wonderful and you just never know. If we had a crystal ball in this business, everyone would be rich. It doesn't work that way. It's the people who decide in the end. Even when all the best minds at work think they've got a wonderful movie, if the populace doesn't like it, it's over. And even if the critics think it's wonderful, if the people don't, it's still over. It'll last for a bit, the lemmings will go along to what the critics tell them to go along to, but it won't be long before everyone says, 'Well that stunk,' and 'What were they smoking when they thought it was good?'"

As it turned out, the initial critical reaction to *A Christmas Story* was mixed. Siskel and Ebert gave the movie "two thumbs up," but other reviewers were less kind.

"*A Christmas Story* no doubt is meant to evoke the lovely sort of Christmas films that were so popular in the late '30s and early '40s, films like *Meet Me in St. Louis* and *Miracle on 34th Street*, but it fails to approximate any of them," John Harkness wrote in his review for *Cinema Canada* in 1984. "I have never been one to complain about the arrival of American productions in this country, nor about the Americans who work in the industry . . . but the time has come to say 'Yankee, go home.'"

"There are a number of small, unexpectedly funny moments in *A Christmas Story*," *New York Times*' Vincent Canby wrote in his review. "But you'd have to possess the stamina of a pearl diver to find them."

Although the critical reaction was hardly worth writing home about, the film did win two Genie Awards, Canada's top film industry honor, for its screenplay and direction.

Since MGM had been so restrained in its spending, *A Christmas Story* was hardly a barn-burning addition to the studio's catalog. Despite the film's modest returns, or perhaps because of them, MGM had a limited re-release of the film during the holiday season of 1984. By that year, the film was beginning to be identified as a financial success; *Variety* even alleged that a sequel was in the works.

The film had its first airing on HBO in 1985, which played a part in the film's growing popularity. But even more significant that year was the film's release on VHS. Thanks to audiences taking a chance at video stores across North America, the film began to make money again. Throughout the following year, the film picked up steam on home video, and *A Christmas Story* began to develop an underground following.

"It was very easy to copy those VHS tapes," actress Tedde Moore explains. "One person would buy the VHS and then give it to all their friends to copy onto theirs. It went a bit like that. It had quite a life."

While the film gained in popularity and attention, MGM found itself in freefall by the following year. The studio was drowning in massive debt, and in early 1986, they sold the bulk of their film library to Hollywood mogul Ted Turner. He began to find ways to capitalize on his newfound library, which, of course, included *A Christmas Story*.

By 1988, the film was on Turner's SuperStation cable channels across the United States during the holiday season. Even without a promotional push or much fanfare, an audience found those broadcasts and Turner, ever the wise businessman, began a holiday tradition.

In December 1990, Turner Network Television (TNT) broadcast *A Christmas Story* during a block of seasonal movies and specials. The airing was a ratings success, and in the years that followed, the film played as part of the regular rotation of holiday programming.

Throughout this time, home video rentals and sales continued to climb, and an underground legion of fans was created. Just as children of the mid-twentieth century had counted down the days till they could watch the annual broadcast of *The Wizard of Oz* over Thanksgiving weekend, fans now caused *A Christmas Story* to slowly and steadily, yet intensely, become television's must-see event of the holiday season.

Before *A Christmas Story* became one of the most revered holiday movies of all time, ownership of the film transferred hands once more. In 1996, Turner Broadcasting System and Time Warner, Inc., the parent company of Warner Bros. Pictures, merged. From that point on, Warner Bros. became the company assigned to dealing with the film in all avenues of release, television rights, and merchandise.

In the mid-1990s, right before the two companies merged, *A Christmas Story* was shown more times on television than ever before. In 1995, the film aired six times from December 24 to 26 on the Turner Broadcasting System, Turner Classic Movies, and Turner Network Television channels. The following year, right after the merger, it had two additional airings.

Those multiple airings were kids' stuff in comparison to what began in 1997. With their newfound acquisition of the Turner library, Time Warner aired the film on a continuous loop from Christmas Eve until Christmas Day on the TNT network. Billed as "24 Hours of *A Christmas Story*," those previously uninitiated with the film could now catch the quirky classic during any one of twelve showings over the holiday.

"We realize *A Christmas Story* has really become over the past ten years the new Christmas classic," Lisa Mateas, an executive at TNT, said at the time. "A lot of people really like this movie, and I'm going to tell you that they didn't see it in the theater; they saw it on television."

The marathon was a ratings success, which led to the twenty-four-hour block becoming a standard practice. By the time Warner Bros. released the twentieth anniversary two-disc special edition DVD set in 2003, the movie was an undeniable juggernaut on the way to reaching the pop stratosphere. The following year, the marathon moved to TNT's sister network, TBS, where it firmly planted its flag as must-see TV during the holiday season.

It wasn't just fans of the film and studio executives who noticed the tide beginning to turn in *A Christmas Story*'s favor. Many of the actors noticed the increased attention to the little film they had made in 1983.

"I *do* watch [the marathon]," Peter Billingsley said in a 2010 interview. "It generally winds up on television in the house for a little bit. Some folks in my family still enjoy that movie very much and I do, too. We watch some little snippets here and there, and then we'll switch to any potential sporting events which may be on. So of the twenty-four-hour marathon, we probably end up watching the whole movie at least once by the end of it."

For Tedde Moore, the film's slow ascent was understandable and to be expected, considering the time period in which the film was released and the way society had changed over the twenty years that followed. "We were in the '80s," she explains. "It was extremely uncool to be innocent, to be naive, to be sweet, to be gentle. These things were out of fashion. Look at the rock 'n' roll at the time. It was grotesque. It was brutish. It was anti-female in the worst possible way, and this was cool. Bob [Clark]'s take on this pure family of happiness and life and innocent time was considered absolutely not on for the time. I think it was cultural."

Over the course of the twenty or so years that followed the film's release, it became apparent that the movie was not only growing in popularity but also becoming inescapable. "A lot of people won't leave me alone. It's a pain in the butt," Bob Clark joked in 2003. "No, that's not true."

Of course, it *was* half-true. It might not have been a pain to be confronted by *Christmas Story* fans, but those who love the movie make sure they unleash platitudes on any members of the cast or crew when they realize their involvement with the picture.

"Every room I've ever walked in as an actor on an audition, or on the set of something, or even as a producer or director, people do tend to recognize me," R.D. Robb, who played Schwartz, said in 2003. "It's definitely a conversation starter."

"I had a flight attendant come up to me once and say, 'Boy, you look so much like the kid from *A Christmas Story*, but you can't be because that movie was shot in the 1940s,'" Peter Billingsley recalls, chuckling.

Super fan Brian Jones hadn't run into any of the actors on a movie set or plane, but he was definitely an admirer of the movie. The film was already a megahit when Jones, a then twenty-eight-year-old in San Diego, noticed the easily identifiable house from *A Christmas Story* for sale on eBay in 2004, but it reached a new level of pop culture infamy when the Californian made a life-changing decision.

"I emailed the guy and said, 'Hey, I want to buy the house. I'm serious,'" Jones recalls. "He emailed me back the next day. His brother owned half of it, so he called his brother and said, 'Hey, can we sell it to this guy?' Within less than twenty-four hours I owned the house. I snatched it up as quickly as I possibly could."

Although the house was being offered on eBay for $99,900, Jones offered the owners $150,000 to cancel the listing and sell it to him outright. They agreed, and he soon found himself not only with the *Christmas Story* house but also in the doghouse.

"My wife was none too impressed," Jones says. "She's actually in the Navy and was on deployment, heading toward the Middle East. I didn't even ask her, I just bought it. It took me all of a day."

Coincidentally, it was Jones' wife who first saw the listing and informed him about it. What had begun as an interesting conversation topic between the two quickly became a potential bludgeon in their relationship.

"When she wrote me and first told me about it, it was in line five of some regular email about how her day was going and, 'Oh, by the way did you see this,'" he says. "Never in her wildest dreams did she think I would go and buy it."

While buying a rundown house halfway across the country from an internet listing sight unseen might have been bad enough, Jones' wife had a more substantial reason to be annoyed with her husband.

"The money I spent on that was actually supposed to be a down payment for our house we planned to buy that year," he confesses. "Now I just blew it all on some rickety old rental property in Cleveland, Ohio. I didn't even know where Cleveland was. I had to look it up on MapQuest."

Although the house listed was the location used for exterior shots of the Parker home, it bore little resemblance to the iconic yellow house with dark green trim that had once provided safe haven to the Old Man's major award. The house, built in 1895, had been refinished with a blue-gray siding and modernized with contemporary windows. While the large porch remained, there was very little left to identify the home as that of the Parkers. Except for one significant detail — in the backyard there was a shed that had barely retained the unmistakable shade of "Christmas Story Yellow."

© David Monseur

Jones' hair-trigger purchase may seem erratic, but that's only if you don't know that his own home was fast becoming a manufacturing and shipping warehouse for a *Christmas Story*–themed startup inspired in large part by a gift his parents had given him a few years earlier.

"Ever since I was a little kid, I wanted to be a jet pilot in the Navy," Jones explains. "My dad flew a plane, so I thought being a pilot was really cool. I studied hard in school, went to the neighborhood academy, and failed the vision test. I got reassigned to be an intelligence officer, which is not even close to being a pilot. That's what I wanted to do all my life, so I was bummed."

To help diffuse his depression, Jones' mom and pop thought a nostalgic present might put a smile on his face. "My parents sent me a leg lamp as a kind of joke gag gift to help me deal with life's disappointments," he continues. With the gift, his parents included a card that read, "It's not all bad. Here's a major award for handling it well." "I asked where they bought it and they had actually made it. It took them a month and a half. They had to go down to the garment district, get a leg. They bought a lampshade from a secondhand store and put it together. I thought it was great and whenever people would come over they'd say, 'Hell yeah, it's the leg lamp from *A Christmas Story*!'"

The gag gift worked and Jones did two tours with the Navy. He owed five years of service as a result of going to naval academy, but as he approached the beginning of his fourth year, he was fed up. *"I didn't sign up to be an intelligence officer,"* he thought. *"I signed up because I wanted to be a pilot."*

Jones wanted to get out of the Navy, but he couldn't decide what he wanted to do. His problem wasn't a shortage of ideas; rather, he had an over-abundance of them. He considered a career in real estate, or perhaps he'd become an accountant. He was too stuck in his own disappointment with his life's direction to realize that the answer to what he should do was sitting in his San Diego condo — the pick-me-up present designed to give renewed inspiration in just these types of downtrodden situations.

"It dawned on me that I should sell leg lamps," Jones says, still sounding just as inspired as he must have been the moment he thought up the idea. "People always liked leg lamps. A buddy of mine who was a science major had just made a website for his dad and was like, 'I'll make you a website.' That was all the push I needed. I formed a little company and figured out how to make leg lamps. I started to glue them together in my condo and sold them on the internet."

Red Ryder Leg Lamps, the name of Jones' new company, began production on April 9, 2003. The company was an immediate success. For $139.99, and a modest shipping and handling fee, Jones would ship a custom-made leg lamp anywhere in the world. Before long, the lamps were available in several independent retailer shops across the United States, and other websites signed on to be authorized resellers of the sexy prop replica.

With his business helping him pay the bills and Jones becoming a pioneer in the large-scale *Christmas Story* merchandising area, it was a no-brainer for him to want to expand the film's presence in the pop culture landscape beyond lamp replicas. The *Christmas Story* House, as it formally became known, was the perfect place to do it.

Early on, the young man who took a chance on purchasing a piece of film history had intended to create a museum inside the house that would be dedicated to the film. The property would, of course, include a gift shop where Jones' lamps could be sold, alongside any other memorabilia from the film he could get for a wholesale price to sell to fans and tourists alike.

Within a day of agreeing to purchase the house, Jones set out to Cleveland to complete paperwork and lay eyes on his new business venture for the first time. The results were less than inspiring. "The place had been a rental property for twenty, twenty-five years since the filming," Jones explains.

© David Monseur

"We pulled an entire dumpster worth of junk out of the basement, just old boxes. The basement flooded a couple times, so if you tried to pick up a box, the bottom fell out and things fell all over the place."

In order to succeed, Jones would have to significantly renovate the house. The siding would have to go in exchange for the late 1930s/early 1940s look of the film. The other significant issue was that the inside of the house in no way resembled what one would expect to see. Because the interior scenes were filmed on a soundstage, the inside of the house was nothing like what fans of the film would expect the Parker family's house to look like. In fact, the house was actually a duplex, a fact that the filmmakers deliberately worked around while shooting to give the appearance that the Parker family lived in a single-family dwelling.

Jones' gamble was about to become even bigger as he prepared to move him and his wife further away from their goal of putting a payment on a San Diego home of their own. "The biggest problem was financing," he explains. "I think I had eight credit cards out at one point to cover [the renovation costs]. I couldn't get a commercial loan because it was residential house and I couldn't get a residential loan because it [was] going to be a commercial property. Nobody would touch it because it wasn't the cookie-cutter situation bankers like to see. This was back in the days of free credit . . . they were just giving them out free, $15,000 here, $20,000 there, so I pulled those cards out, hoping that by the time [the house] opened it would do well so I'd be able to pay the credit cards off before I had any interest."

Even after kicking in the profits from Red Ryder Leg Lamps, Jones took a giant leap off a financial cliff and hoped that a safety net would be waiting for him at the bottom. Overall, the house that was initially listed for just under $100,000 ended up costing over $240,000 after renovations. "It would've been easier to build a house from the ground up instead of renovating but nobody wants to come to 'The Rebuilt *Christmas Story* House,'" Jones says. "They want to come to the original renovated one."

Renovations began on January 30, 2006, and concluded nearly ten months later. In order to make the house appear to be the same as the soundstage set, a staircase was constructed, a bedroom replaced, and the entire home was outfitted with furniture that was as close to the screen-used props as he could find. Jones and his teams left no detailed unturned, down to the *Little Orphan Annie* decoder pin and Lifebuoy soap in the Parker bathroom.

© Jesse Yost

© David Monseur

eBay also ended up being instrumental in Jones' expansion of his business venture and in getting the attention of cast members of *A Christmas Story*. "Scott Schwartz's dad owned a baseball cards and movie collectibles store which used to be in Westlake Village, California, and from sixth grade on, I grew up in Newbury Park, which is two towns over," Jones begins. "I think I was in junior high. My mom was in some boring store that was by his dad's store, so my dad [took] my sister and me to the collectible store. I [was] dorking around, looking at stuff, and there was a poster up of Scott. I said, 'I think that's the kid from *Kidco*,'" and his dad, Dan, said, 'That's my son. He's also in *A Christmas Story*.'

"Years later, when I was starting to sell leg lamps, I saw this listing on eBay of a little miniature leg lamp signed by Scott Schwartz," Jones continues. "I knew that had to be Scott selling his own stuff, so I approached him and said, 'Hey, would you be interested in signing some stuff,' and he was like, 'I don't know. I'll think about it.'"

Jones wasn't the only person who had tried to do *Christmas Story* business with Schwartz that year. Before the previous owner had put the house on eBay, he had attempted to get in contact with the actor to offer him the opportunity to buy it. Ultimately, the two never connected. As Jones remembers it, the owner attempted to catch Schwartz at a public appearance, but the actor had left early. Regardless of the reason, the owner decided to roll the dice on the internet instead of continuing to chase Schwartz.

After Jones purchased the house, he went back to the store for a second time to see the actor. "Hey, I bought the house," Jones said. "Would you be interested in being part of it?"

"What do you mean?"

"I don't know. Come out for fundraisers, cast signings? You could make some money signing autographs."

Schwartz was still in touch with some of the other film actors, especially since the group had recently reconvened for the twentieth anniversary screening of the film in 2003. He reached out to Zack Ward and Ian Petrella. Jones found Tedde Moore and Yano Anaya on the internet. Patty Johnson and Drew Hocevar were locals who still lived in the Cleveland area and were quick to reach out to Jones once they heard the house was going to be converted into a tourist attraction.

"I saw an article in *The Plain Dealer* about this guy and the *Christmas Story* House before he had even done anything with it," Patty Johnson says. "He had just purchased the house and didn't know what he was going to do with it yet. After I read the article, I emailed him and said, 'I'm the elf from Hell and still live in Cleveland, if you're interested.' Of course, he got back to me right away. I knew how to get ahold of Drew and when we started to discuss press and events, we were involved from early on because we were local."

"One thing just led to another," Jones says.

The entrepreneur invited the cast to the house over Thanksgiving weekend in 2005 to participate in a three-day fundraiser to help defer the costs of the overhaul project. The weekend, which included tours of the house before renovations, a downtown parade, and tree lighting ceremony, among other activities, extended beyond the block where the house and museum are located. Tower City Cinemas, a local movie house in Cleveland, held a screening of the film and the Renaissance Cleveland Hotel had a display of movie memorabilia.

Even though catching one of the first glimpses of the *Christmas Story* House would have made the trip worth it for Tedde Moore, she had the added benefit

Scott Schwartz signs autographs
© David Monseur

of celebrating her first American Thanksgiving in Cleveland that weekend.

"I was picked up at the airport by Brian and swept off to have a Thanksgiving dinner at the home of the parents of his [business] partner, *Christmas Story* House curator Steve Siedlecki," she recalls. "It was a wonderful meal, very lovingly prepared by his family, with *A Christmas Story* on the TV in the background."

For the remaining members of the cast, the weekend also proved to be a memorable experience. "I remember when Brian first bought the place," Petrella says. "We [the actors] went down to see it and it was obvious he needed a lot of help. My mom had taken candid pictures on the soundstage, and I was able to lend those to him to help him out."

The pictures proved to be invaluable in helping Jones achieve the level of accuracy that he hoped for. "If you look at the house, and you look at certain pieces of furniture in it, and you look at the movie, he nailed it," Petrella states. "As far as capturing the look and feel of the movie, he really came through as far as I'm concerned. It's sort of like Fantasy Island for *A Christmas Story*. You can come in and reenact your own scenes as much as you want."

Zack Ward (left) and Ian Petrella (right) tour the *Christmas Story* House with Yano Anaya's son before the grand opening © Brian Jones

"I've got family out in Akron, Ohio," Zack Ward explains. "So when we went out there I thought, 'Okay, free ticket. We'll do some press for the house and nothing will really come of it. I'll be able to go see my buddy and my little nieces.' And when we got there, there were literally close to 10,000 people lined up and it was a little more than overwhelming."

Patty Johnson echoes Ward's sentiments. As a Cleveland local, she continues to find it astonishing that she can walk down the street and be virtually anonymous a mile away from the house, but once she gets within striking distance of that block, she's a rock star. "When we had that first reunion, I kept thinking no one was going to come," she says. "I thought it was just going to be us sitting down there like a bunch of jamokes. I had no idea, absolutely no idea. It was just stunning to me. I feel like I have my real life, where I'm taking out the garbage and schlepping stuff to and from school, and my surreal life, where I'm signing autographs all day and having thousands of pictures taken of me. It's an interesting phenomenon."

For Yano Anaya, his appearances with the other *Christmas Story* actors are more about camaraderie than the feeling of fame. "The reason why I get back with these guys is because we've created a bond which is very similar to brothers now," he says.

For Zack Ward, the most overwhelming moment came during the weekend's holiday parade. "We were in these sleighs with wheels being pulled around by horses around the square, and I'm wearing my Scut Farkus hat, and as we're being pulled around, I'm waving," he says. "I don't do parades. I don't know what to do, so I'm sort of doing the queen's wave. I think about it and realize, *Scut Farkus doesn't wave at children. Scut Farkus beats the hell out of children.* I saw a kid in a crowd and I made a fist and punched my other hand, like 'You! I'm gonna beat your ass!' The kid squealed and got the biggest smile on his face and his mom was like, 'Yeah! Get him,' so I yelled, 'Who wants a beatin'?' All these mothers started holding up their children for me to threaten. 'You! I'm coming for you!' I'm a loved abuser of children, what can I say? I thought that was the most bizarre, funny, interesting thing."

Drew Hocevar (left) and Patty Johnson (right) meet a fan
© David Monseur

The Grand Marshall for the parade that year was none other than international pop star Tom Jones, who previously had been acquainted with Tedde Moore. "I met Sir Tom Jones, as he is now known, for the first time when I was attending the Royal Academy of Dramatic Arts in London," she recalls. "It was 1965 and I was seventeen. He couldn't have been much older, as he was just starting his career. A strapping young fellow, he was truly poured into his shiny powder blue suit. His trademark was wearing these very tight pants and I can assure you they were tight. So tight, in fact, that he couldn't sit down and had to take his tea standing up at the bar."

Tedde Moore with fan
Michael Kopatich
© Michael Kopatich

Although she was a casual observer of his career, Jones' music didn't really interest her. She never could have imagined that she would wind up meeting him again, standing side-by-side with him in the middle of Cleveland on a frigid morning in November. "You may not remember this, but we've met before," she said before recalling the story for him in the middle of Cleveland's main square.

"Sounds like that was a long time ago," he said with a polite smile.

As incongruous as it may have seemed for the cast to be appearing in a parade headlined by Tom Jones, it actually made a lot of sense. Like the Super Bowl, the Grammy Awards, and the Times Square celebration on New Year's Eve, *A Christmas Story* transcends age, race, and gender. It still brings people together from all walks of life around the globe.

On November 25, 2006, just over a month after the final renovations were made on the house, several cast members made the trek back to middle America to help celebrate the grand opening of the completely restored house. On a day cold enough to make your eyes tear, Yano Anaya, Ian Petrella, Scott Schwartz, Drew Hocevar, Patty Johnson, Tedde Moore, and Zack Ward greeted several thousand well-bundled fans who wanted to be among the first to catch a glimpse of the supporting cast from their favorite holiday film.

Yano Anaya arrived at the opening day ceremony with his son, who now bears a striking resemblance to Grover Dill. "People used to tell him all the time that he looked like that kid in *A Christmas Story*," he says with a laugh. "Imagine their surprise when he told them 'that kid' was his dad!"

Darren McGavin in 1990
© Photofest

The festivities continued throughout the weekend, with a convention that included a screening of the film. Thousands of glossy 8x10s with sprawling Sharpie marker signatures transferred from the hands of the former child actors, most of whom still bore an uncanny resemblance to their pre-pubescent versions that appeared on screen, to the eager fans who couldn't wait to race back to their homes and put the picture next to their television or under their Christmas tree.

The success of the opening weekend even turned around the person who was among the first to express doubt over whether the venture would be a success. "My wife thought that selling the lamps was going to be a hobby," Jones said in a 2005 interview. "After I got out of the Navy, she kept asking, 'When are you going to get a job . . . you know, a J-O-B?' But she's warming to the lamp idea — and the house — now."

According to Tyler Schwartz, the Canadian distributor for Jones' leg lamps, the house doesn't just attract attention during the holiday season. This is likely due to the warm embrace the attraction has received from two important entities. "I dropped by there fairly recently, mid-summer, and this time I happened to take my dad because I wanted to show him what all the fuss was about," Schwartz says. "We dropped by and there was a line out the door. My dad said, 'What the heck is going on,' and I told him there are only two attractions in Cleveland: the Rock and Roll Hall of Fame and this. If you're in the Cleveland area, you've gotta come.

"The fact that the guy bought the house on eBay without knowing anything about bylaws, without knowing whether or not you can run a tourist attraction in the middle of a residential neighborhood, is astonishing to me," he continues. "Any other town in the United States would have said, 'No way,' but Cleveland is so hard up for anything that they said, go ahead. That's the most incredible thing. Warner Bros. could have said 'F.U.,' but instead of getting up in arms, they said, 'Okay, slap our logo on it, give us a couple bucks for every person who walks through the door,' and it just kind of worked out."

Of course, not all the *Christmas Story* cast was present and accounted for that day. Darren McGavin had passed away earlier that year following two strokes. Melinda Dillon, who has maintained steady work as an actress, has

opted to avoid discussing the film since its release. R.D. Robb, who played the smartass Schwartz, has also limited his *Christmas* activities.

"R.D. hasn't come around with us," Scott Schwartz says. "He's been very lucky in life. He married a wonderful, absolutely gorgeous, beautiful woman who is an executive for a distribution company, and she makes so much money. He doesn't work all that much. He writes. He tries to get some indie films done, but he doesn't even have to work, realistically. He takes care of their baby, and their [older] child, and he's enjoying life."

However, there is one other person who has spent the last ten years walking a delicate line between being one of the film's biggest cheerleaders and one of its most absent cast members at public appearances. Peter Billingsley, who had long since shed his baby fat and traded his mahogany-tinted round eyeglasses for contact lenses, was also missing from the opening day celebration. Ralphie may not have come home on that date, but it wouldn't be too long before he returned to the forefront of the choir singing the film's praises.

Zack Ward, Yano Anaya (with his son), Tedde Moore, Ian Petrella, Scott Schwartz, Patty Johnson, and Drew Hocevar reunited at the *Christmas Story* House grand opening © Brian Jones

CHAPTER SIX

Explorers
Road Trip
for Ralphie

In **The Truman Show,** the 1998 comedy-drama starring Jim Carrey, there's a brief flashback intended to explain why Truman Burbank, the film's protagonist, hasn't attempted to venture outside of his city limits.

"And what do you want to be when you grow up?" his teacher asked.

"I want to be an explorer, like the Great Magellan!"

"Oh, you're too late," his teacher replied as she pulled down a scrolling map. "There's nothing left to explore."

Tyler and Jordie Schwartz
© Tyler Schwartz

While this moment is played for laughs, there is a grain of truth to the teacher's claim. Many rebuke independent research because, in the Wikipedia age, everything that can be found out about a topic must already be online. If it isn't easily found on a Google search, it couldn't possibly exist.

Tyler Schwartz, a longtime fan of *A Christmas Story*, doesn't subscribe to that thinking. Like Christopher Columbus centuries before him, he is a great explorer who, in 2005, set out to discover some of the long-lost history behind one of his favorite films. "Before the museum and house in Cleveland even opened, I saw what Brian Jones was doing and I thought it was super-cool," Tyler explains. "And I thought, 'Okay, that's a part of the story. What about the Canadian locations where the rest of the movie — where most of the movie — was shot? Most of the interiors were shot on a soundstage in Toronto, not in Cleveland. If you combine the clips and footage that [were] shot in Cleveland, you're talking about five, ten minutes."

His assessment is largely correct. Principal photography on *A Christmas Story* lasted nine weeks, only two of which were spent in Cleveland. Not only was the Midwestern city only briefly used, but a number of sequences, like when Randy falls down in the snow and the "Oh, fudge" scene by the bridge, were originally shot in Cleveland but had to be done over in Toronto because the footage wasn't good enough to print.

For Tyler, as a Canadian, the mythology that the film's roots traced back to the States was somewhat confusing and mildly perturbing. With the house soon to become a tourist attraction, Tyler, along with his wife, Jordie, embarked on a two-year-long quest to trace down filming locations and uncover any lost treasures along the way. Early on, a decision was made to videotape their adventures, which led to the independent documentary, *Road Trip for Ralphie*.

There was a certain level of brazenness required to decide to take on a documentary film project. By Tyler's own admission, the Schwartzes aren't filmmakers and their crew consisted of nothing more than Tyler behind a run-of-the-mill camcorder, and his wife, who Tyler says is "gifted with natural presence," as the talent. How did this idea come about and what inspired the dynamic duo to set off on this adventure?

The answer lies in Cleveland, as so many *Christmas* stories do. "It really was started by my admiration for what Brian Jones was doing for the house," Tyler explains. "I had a boring desk job and somehow I got on Brian's email list. When he first bought the house he would do a monthly email blast updating everyone about how the renovations were going. I became so enamored with this stuff."

With renewed interest in the film, Tyler became a *Christmas Story* magnet. If something turned up online, he would bookmark the page and share it with his wife. When Jones sent out a new email, he would sneakily read it at his computer desk, anxious to see how the project was progressing and astonished that Jones had the audacity to take on this endeavor in the first place. "He's a great guy," Tyler says. "He's the American Dream in person. He had this great idea, and the fact that it has worked out for him is partly because he has balls and partly because he has great luck."

But Jones' luck had yet to be tested. The *Christmas Story* House was still under renovation when, during the holiday season of 2005, a happy accident occurred that kickstarted the Schwartzes' two-year quest. The couple was watching *A Christmas Story* on television and saw the name of the shop that had provided the costumes for the film. Out of curiosity, Tyler typed the name into Google and was pleasantly surprised to see that it was still in existence. He called and spoke to a woman, the same woman who had outfitted the actors for the film, in fact, and asked if she still had the pieces they had used on-screen. She did, and Tyler booked an appointment to go down and see them. "She must have just thought I was a crazy fan," he says. "She had no idea what she had in there."

Jordie and Tyler Schwartz © Tyler Schwartz

Costumes on display at the *Christmas Story* House Museum © Jesse Yost

Tyler arrived early one morning with his wife and a bunch of screen-shots printed out from his home computer. What they found wasn't only jaw-dropping but downright intimidating. There were several floors of costumes separated by type, each rack filled to capacity with garments. The Schwartzes had hoped that there might be a special section designated to *A Christmas Story*, or at least that the costumer would know where those specific pieces were, but that wasn't the case.

Tyler and his wife made their way through the racks systematically, and within hours scored some significant finds. In the section marked "Men's Jackets," they found the gray tweed coat that Darren McGavin's Old Man wore in the film. Elsewhere, in the "Ladies' Morning Clothes" area, Melinda Dillon's Christmas nightgown turned up. Randy's unforgettable red snow-suit, the one made famous by the scene in which his mother bundles him up so tightly from the cold that he can't put his arms down, turned up in the "Boys' Jackets" region.

For all the great finds that were scored that first day, one item was nowhere to be found. "We couldn't find Ralphie's jacket because it was out on loan," Tyler says. "The costumer had lost track of the fact that *A Christmas*

Story had become this cult movie. She just thought of it as a little flop of a film that was made a long time ago. I told her she really had something on her hands. People have asked me why I didn't just downplay it and try and buy everything for ten bucks, but that's not my style."

They left that day having identified a few armfuls of costumes. The costumer agreed to put them on hold for the couple, even though they didn't yet have any idea what to do with their find. They returned several times, finding more and more pieces from the film and putting them aside, snapping photographs as they progressed. Before long, they had traced down nearly every costume piece that the costumer had provided for the film, including the aforementioned jacket worn by Ralphie.

Days turned into weeks and weeks into months, and all the while Tyler and Jordie tried to figure out what to do with their collection of photographs

© David Monseur

and the pile of costumes that sat in the large, cold warehouse. *"These have to be seen,"* Tyler thought. *"But how? Where? And who's going to be the right person to make this happen?"*

Tyler and Jordie Schwartz hold the jacket worn by the character Schwartz in the film © Tyler Schwartz

Ian Petrella's zeppelin
donated to the *Christmas
Story* House Museum
© David Monseur

Of course, Brian Jones was the answer. They sent him an email letting him know of their find, and he replied back promptly. He was interested — so much so that he booked a trip to Canada to take a look for himself.

The Schwartzes' initial idea was for the costumer to loan the *Christmas Story* House the costume pieces for an extended period of time. According to Tyler, the museum was badly in need of some more material to make the trip worthwhile to the tourists who were, by now, coming from miles around to see the property.

"By the time Brian got there, we had pulled them all together into one collection," Tyler says. "He had already opened the museum. There were some things Ian [Petrella] had loaned the museum, but Brian was in need of more to make it an actual experience."

When the American made his trek over the country's northern border, he was amazed at what he saw. *"These costumes shouldn't make a temporary stay in the museum,"* he thought. *"Cleveland has to be their permanent home."* He met with the costumer and made his intentions known. "Brian made her an offer she couldn't refuse, and within five minutes, they were his," Tyler says. "She was flabbergasted. She thought they were all practically worthless."

Jones packed up his pieces and made his way back to Cleveland. To this day, the costumes continue to generate much interest at his museum — his investment has paid off quite handsomely.

The explorers turned their attention to St. Catharines to see Victoria Public School, the place immortalized on celluloid as Warren G. Harding Elementary. Unfortunately, while the school lives forever on film, it did not in reality. In January 2005, the school closed. The Schwartzes discovered that the building was sold for over a million dollars for the purposes of being converted into a women's shelter. Tyler made a telephone call to the woman in charge at the purchasing organization.

(Top left) Victoria Public School © Anne Dean (Top right) Jordie Schwartz restoring Miss Shields' chalkboard © Tyler Schwartz (Bottom) Jordie and Tyler Schwartz with Tedde Moore and the restored chalkboard © Cindy Jones

"Hi, I'm Tyler Schwartz," he said before explaining why he was calling. "Is anything left in the school? Maybe the blackboard used in the classroom where they shot the movie? The one where the teacher wrote 'A+++++++?'"

"Yeah, everything's still inside," she said. "But we're gutting it tomorrow. If you wanna come down and grab whatever you want, you can."

The next day, armed with a sledgehammer, crowbar, and their old reliable camcorder, Tyler and Jordie appeared in sweatshirts to brave the cold and contribute to the demolition. Although they were happy to be there, others were less thrilled by their presence. "There were a lot of annoyed-looking people," Tyler says. "I'm pretty sure we just got in their way."

Before long, they had found the blackboard that, if not for their serendipitous telephone call twenty-four hours earlier, would have ended up exiled to an anonymous garbage dump somewhere in Ontario. The two also took various knickknacks — like the coat hooks and door trim — and endured the stares of some of the volunteers who were helping. "People were looking at us like, 'Why are you trying to save this?'" Tyler says. "But thank God we did!" The items made their way into their van and within a few months to the museum in Cleveland.

Before they left, though, the Schwartzes visited the field where Flick had fallen victim to the triple-dog-dare. When the school was sold to the organization converting it into a woman's shelter, they also sold off the field to a developer to recoup some of the costs. Townhouses soon started to spring up onto what was formerly school property. When the Schwartzes arrived in 2006, most of the plots had already been sold, but the spot that had once been the focal point of a frosty January shoot was left undisturbed.

"The flagpole lot was on sale until recently," Schwartz said in 2012. He had been tempted to buy it, but met some resistance from his partner. "My wife wouldn't go for it. She said there are limits. There's a house there now and I wonder if they're aware that they're literally sitting on a holy grail of film history."

The scene where the Parkers purchase their Christmas tree was shot in Canada © Ian Petrella

When the Victoria Public School closed, the previous owners didn't know what to do with all of the trophies, awards, and other artifacts that had been collected over time. In the school's last days, it was decided that all of the belongings would be donated to another school, down the street, for safekeeping. The time capsule with the *Christmas Story* script signed by Peter Billingsley and Tedde Moore, as well as the Betamax copy of the director's cut of the film, was dug up and its contents were sent a few blocks away. In his quest to uncover the items, Tyler made his way down to the school.

"I never actually saw the video, but I was assured it was there," he says. "I held the script in my hands, though. They kept it in a safe in the principal's office. Of course, they wouldn't let me keep it."

A year later he was curious enough to make another trip down to the school to see if they would part with the script or the video. The unfortunate reality was that they already had. "They had no idea what I was talking about," he said. "They had gotten a new principal who threw out everything from Victoria School. They just didn't know where to put it all." In an instant, the chances of ever seeing the truly rare footage became even more diminished.

But the search for long-lost *Christmas Story* locations continued. The Schwartzes obtained copies of the filming permits from the Toronto Film

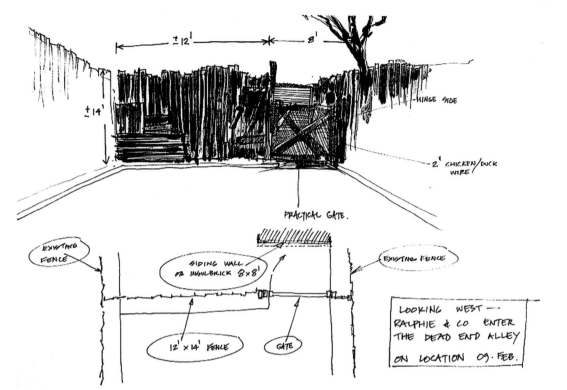

Production designer Reuben Freed's original sketch of the alley location © Reuben Freed

Reference Library, which led them on several successful expeditions. On Sears Street they found the alleyway where Scut Farkus chased Ralphie and his friends, and the lot where the bully was beat up as the protagonist muttered unspeakable obscenities. On Queen Street East at St. Patrick Square, they found the lot where the Parkers had purchased their Christmas tree. Near the Cherry Street Bridge, they found the location where the queen mother of dirty words was uttered.

The permits led the Schwartzes to one other location that had evaded them: the Chop Suey Palace where the Parkers had Chinese Christmas dinner at the end of the film. Before getting the permits, the duo had driven all around Toronto, hoping to see a building that they recognized. A piece of anecdotal history from the shooting further complicated their quest.

In the movie, the sign on the building says "Bo Ling," but it's clear that another letter, not glowing pink, is connecting those two words. Rumor had it that location manager Michael MacDonald had found a restaurant to shoot in that was attached to a bowling alley. When their aimless driving around proved to be unfruitful, the Schwartzes took to the yellow pages to search not only for Chinese restaurants but also for bowling alleys. It ended up being a wild goose chase.

According to Brian Jones, the inspiration for the visual joke was inspired by a childhood memory of Ken Goch, the assistant director on the film. His mother had once taken him to a bowling alley that had a sign with a burnt out "w" because she thought it was a Chinese restaurant. Before filming began on the scene, the story was recounted to Bob Clark, who requested a similar sign be placed on the exterior of the restaurant where they'd be shooting.

When the Schwartzes used the information provided on the permits to make their way to the restaurant, the reason they had previously had difficulty finding it became obvious. The eatery, located at 744 Gerrard Street East in Toronto, was now a café that served French cuisine, not Chinese as depicted in the movie. The new owners were just as surprised to find that their location was the site where Ralphie and his family had heard a rousing rendition of "Deck the Halls" from a host of Chinese waiters.

As the Schwartzes were discovering long-lost shooting locations, Tyler mused about what it would be like to create a Canadian equivalent of the *Christmas Story* House Museum. He wished he could have purchased the Chinese restaurant before it was sold, just as he still wishes he could turn back time and put in a bid for Victoria Public School.

"I've daydreamed about it a lot," he says. "I wish I could have gotten to that school before it was sold to the women's shelter, but who am I kidding? I couldn't have afforded to buy an entire school anyway, so that wouldn't have worked."

Even without realizing his dream of building a Canadian museum, Tyler
has found a venue to keep his love for the film alive and also spread some
Christmas cheer. When Brian Jones made his way to purchase the costumes
for his museum, he told the explorer that he needed someone to help distrib-
ute leg lamps and other film-related merchandise on that side of the border
in Canada, because Jones believed potential international customers were
deterred by high shipping costs.

"He mentioned to me that they weren't selling anything in Canada
because of the shipping costs," Tyler says. "He needed a distributor. At some
point he approached Tedde Moore about it. She declined, although she was
intrigued."

Within a few years, the business took off to the extent that Tyler could
leave his boring desk job behind. Today, he drives around in a car with a van-
ity license plate that reads "LEGLAMP," an homage to not only his favorite
movie but also his new career.

The Schwartzes' journey culminated in *Road Trip for Ralphie*. The movie was produced on DVD and is available for purchase at the *Christmas Story* House in Cleveland, as well as on Tyler's website for the Canadian distribution of merchandise inspired by the film. "We get emails about it all the time," he says. "I'm very self-conscious about it. I know it's not a professional documentary, but I think people get it. We're just two fans who had a passion for the movie and set out to make a film for the fans." *Christmas Story* fans don't seem to be bothered by what Tyler describes as the amateur production values in *Ralphie*. Instead, they enjoy the unique experience of being able to enjoy their favorite holiday film in a new and creative way.

For those in the Cleveland area, another new and creative way to experience their favorite film was on the horizon. Once again, it would be Brian Jones who was the catalyst for a most surreal experience for one of the film's actors, as well as the fans lucky enough to interact with him.

CHAPTER SEVEN

This Little Piggy
Came Home

California: the state with Hollywood's brightest stars, those looking to make it big in the entertainment industry . . . and Ian Petrella. After appearing in *A Christmas Story* as Randy Parker, Ralphie's kid brother, Ian continued acting for a few years. Throughout the mid-1980s he made appearances on popular sitcoms like *Diff'rent Strokes* and *Who's the Boss*, but by 1991, he was virtually retired from show business.

By the spring of 2003, Ian was working hard at his latest steady gig, refilling the sugars and cream at a Starbucks, and not thinking too much

© Ian Petrella

about the holiday movie he had filmed when he was nine. He had noticed the growing popularity of *A Christmas Story* and the increased airings on television, but for the most part, the film was off his radar until a few weeks before the annual marathon.

While he was straightening the milk containers at work, he happened to glance up and notice the person beside him. "There was this girl standing next to me, mixing her coffee, and there I was, in my little Starbucks apron," he recalls. "I looked over. She was pretty cute, so I gave her a glance. That's when I noticed her shirt."

He noticed that she was wearing a shirt with President George W. Bush on it, but instead of being dressed in a suit, the president was wearing Ralphie's pink bunny outfit. Ian was surprised, but thought nothing of it. After all, this was ultra-liberal San Francisco, so the actor-turned-barista assumed the shirt was purchased on the street, or maybe at some anti-Bush rally.

But then he looked closer. "I realized it wasn't Bush," Ian says. "It was Peter in a bunny suit and it said 'Pink Nightmare' on it! That was the first time that I saw any merchandise with *A Christmas Story* on it. Anything."

Perhaps a less passionate man would have introduced himself to the woman as the actor in the film. After all, it was safe to deduce that she was a fan and that meeting one of the actors from the movie, especially one as integral as a member of the Parker family, would have made a lasting impression on the customer. Instead, Petrella, who is far from lacking in passion, chose to make a *different* kind of lasting impression.

"I literally grabbed this girl by the arm, spun her around, and said, 'Where the fuck did you get that shirt,'" he explains. "Now, of course, she has no idea who I am. She didn't know I was Randy in the film. She kind of flipped out on me. 'I got it at Hot Topic, asshole,' she said. 'Leave me alone!'"

When his shift ended and Ian returned home, he took to the internet to see if he could find the shirt on Hot Topic's website. He hadn't heard of any officially licensed merchandise and thought maybe the woman had been joking when she said she bought the shirt there. Finally, though, he found the shirt — and more. Lots more.

"All this stuff was being sold," he explains, still sounding surprised by it. "Action figures, leg lamps, everything. This was coming out of the twenty-year anniversary. Nothing was really happening with the film and now, all of a sudden, there's a whole merchandising line."

As Ian sat in front of his computer and looked at the merchandise featuring pictures of himself when he was nine years old, he couldn't help but think about all of those fans who had made the movie a sleeper hit that had only grown in popularity with each passing Christmas season over the last twenty years — and his thoughts were of the worst possible outcome from this scenario.

"*Merchandising will kill this film's cult status,*" he thought. "*All of this stuff will make the movie uncool.*"

He waited for the bottom to fall out from underneath what he perceived to be a misguided and self-serving cash grab by Warner Bros. but that day never came. A few years came and went, and by early 2010, the Californian had transitioned into a budding career in graphic design and production. The problem was, gigs were sparse and the rent on his apartment was high. He needed a breakout opportunity, which came in the form of a telephone call from Brian Jones, the owner of the *Christmas Story* House.

Jones called just to shoot the breeze. The two had become friends after Ian and a number of the other actors from the film had participated in events to promote the Cleveland attraction, and a random telephone call to or from the entrepreneur became fairly commonplace over time.

Ian while filming *A Christmas Story* © Ian Petrella

"What's going on with you?" Jones' question was more a formality than a genuine inquiry, but for Ian, it provided a chance to air some mild frustrations with the direction of his career. He told Jones he was looking for a new apartment and work. San Francisco wasn't working out, and he was eager for a new experience.

"If you're looking for a job and a place to live," Jones said, "why don't you move into the *Christmas Story* House and give tours?"

The suggestion was delivered and received as a joke, but after the phone call ended, the question rang in Ian's ears. After giving it some thought, he called Jones back and said he was interested in giving it a shot.

They decided that Ian would move into the house that summer, an idea that initially seemed like a suicide mission to the actor. Because the film is set during the holiday season, the actor thought attendance would be low during the warmer months. In fact, he didn't even realize the house was open year-round prior to receiving the offer. But Jones assured him that Ian's visit would be worth the nearly 2,500-mile journey to middle America.

Ian Petrella relaxes on the set between takes. © Ian Petrella

That June, the actor packed up his apartment, moved a bunch of things into storage, filled his suitcases, and set off for Cleveland. While the first two floors of the house are open to the public, there's a loft on the third level with a suitable living space that is off-limits to visitors.

The actor wasn't the first person to sleep at the tourist attraction. In 2009, Billy Jeffrey, a former reality television show contestant and Chippendales exotic dancer, made headlines for scoring a stay at the house after bidding $4,200 for the honor in an online charity auction. The following year, while Ian was staying at the house, Jerry Benya, another fan of the film, won a similar overnight stay on Christmas Eve for $3,200. However, as Randy's real-life counterpart was already occupying the loft, Benya slept in Ralphie and Randy's bedroom.

The upper-level of the house could hardly be considered the lap of luxury. First and foremost, the home is a tourist attraction, not a hotel. The loft and house aren't wired for internet access, which means anyone staying there would have to visit a nearby café or the library whenever they needed to check their email. When he arrived, Ian found a bed, television, DVD player, and some movies awaiting him. He perused through his few selections and hoped he'd find something worth watching on the eve of his homecoming.

The first film on the stack was, of course, *A Christmas Story*. He had seen it too many times and certainly wasn't enthusiastic about watching it again on the upper floor of the film's Graceland. *My Summer Story*, the 1994 follow-up to the holiday film, was also there. Ian had seen it and, while he thought it was enjoyable enough, he wasn't particularly in the mood. The third movie, *National Lampoon's Christmas Vacation*, was a film the actor liked, and he probably would have ended up watching it had he not looked at the DVD case on the bottom of the pile — *Elf*.

© Brian Jones

As the only film of the four that Ian hadn't seen before, *Elf* won the draw. He changed his clothes, put on the movie, and got into bed. When the opening credits read "Produced by Peter Billingsley," it was a surreal moment for Cleveland's newest temporary resident. "Life is really fucking weird right now," he said out loud to himself. "That's all there is to it."

The next morning, the test run of tours began. Jones and his team had crafted an aggressive promotional campaign to announce that Ian would be staying at the house. "Randy Comes Home," as they called it, was scheduled to begin in July, but it was decided that the actor should spend the last few weeks of June giving the occasional tour so he'd be up to speed by the next month.

As the clock neared 10 a.m. and people started to line up outside, the actor was still uncertain as to what he was supposed to do. He hadn't been given any guidelines or handbook; he was just advised to live in the house and interact with the visitors as he saw fit. However, even with this supposed freedom, Ian still knew that he had to figure out a way to properly integrate himself into the well-oiled machine that was the *Christmas Story* House. The regular guides were still in charge of directing the tour, so it would be redundant to do that. He decided to let the guides do their thing while he took a backseat during the first test run.

As the group came in, the guides went into their brief spiel. Once again, Ian was acutely caught off guard. The employee gave a one-minute overview of how the film was made, spent a few more talking about how Jones acquired the house, and then finished it up with a little bit of biographical information about the lead actors. "*Where are the interesting anecdotes,*" Ian thought. "*Where are the funny stories about the house's history?*"

Although the interesting anecdotes were missing from the tour, there were several interesting stories to tell. According to Steve Siedlecki, the curator of the house and museum, there was a misunderstanding back in 1982 when location scouts approached the tenant living in the home about filming there. "The guy thought they were cops and he ended up flushing about $5,000 worth of drugs down the toilet," he says.

The crew began their pitch to the resident and, after a very short while, the man realized his error. He agreed to stay in a hotel for two weeks so the crew could use his house for filming. At the time, there was an empty lot nearby that could be used for lights and other equipment, which made the house a perfect choice for the Christmas Tree Films team. Since he was displaced, the tenant with the drug habit was properly compensated — he received $5,000, which potentially made up for his lost narcotics.

After the guide completed his tour, Ian was introduced. Without knowing what to do, he walked up the yellow staircase with the tourists and showed them the rooms, giving brief stories about what it was like to film the scenes on the Toronto soundstage and how interesting it was to be back home. When he had finished giving his supplemental walk-through, an impromptu question and answer session broke out. Ian welcomed the opportunity to fill in the blanks for some of the film's fans, and he spent the next fifteen minutes answering the questions thrown his way.

Ian Petrella poses with fans Shelley, Corbyn, Taelor, and Wyatt Cook
© Shelley Cook

With that, the Ian Petrella Q&A was born. After the guides gave their speech on subsequent tours, they would direct the visitors to find the actor upstairs, where he would be waiting and willing to answer questions for the duration of the session. "There were no guidelines," he says. "Everyone just said, 'Well, let's see what happens.' Whenever you enter a situation like that, that's when it's going to become the most interesting thing possible."

While the idea was inspired in the beginning, the novelty soon began to wear off a bit. Ian needed to come up with a way to keep his shtick fun for him and his audience. "People would ask the same questions over and over again, which comes with the territory," he says. "It got to the point where I would take these questions and develop a comedy routine around them. I'd come up with answers to make everybody laugh."

The jokes were well received by the tourists, even when they were the butt of them. One encounter that sticks out for Ian is when a tour consisted only of a man, his wife, and their children. "The smaller the group, the more difficult your time there is going to be in terms of doing a Q&A," he says. "It's harder to engage people, so I had to think of something."

Ian asked if anybody had any questions. The father, who was standing

against the wall in the living room, muttered, "I can't get up," in reference to the scene in the film when Randy is pushed into the snow and rolls around like a flipped turtle because of his obtrusive snow suit. However innocent the man's intentions were, Ian saw an opening and chose to exploit it.

"That sounds like a personal problem, sir." The man burst out laughing immediately. Emboldened by the reaction, Ian continued. "Maybe you oughta talk to a doctor about that."

The man endured five or six other "limp-dick jokes," as Ian likes to call them, laughing hysterically as they kept coming. When the session was over, the actor approached the man.

"Hey, I hope I didn't offend you."

"No, no, it was fine."

"I'm glad it was all in fun," Ian said. "It really made my day so far."

"No, *you* made *my* day. *A Christmas Story* is my favorite movie in the entire world and today's my birthday!"

As it turned out, his family had surprised him with a visit to the house to celebrate and, even though the jokes were racy, they all got a kick out of them. Ian asked the man for his name and gave him a bunch of signed pictures, free of charge, as a birthday present. The experience has lasted with Ian, and he hopes it's lasted with the family as well. "That easily could have turned into a bad situation, with me making erectile dysfunction jokes in front of his family," he says. "But it didn't. It worked out and everyone really had fun."

But was there ever a concern that tourists, whether they were venturing to the house with their children or not, would be bothered by hearing Ian Petrella uncensored? For the actor, it was all a part of what made the experience distinctive for the visitors.

"As far as I was concerned, I'm Ian Petrella and that's all there is to it," he says. "I have a certain personality and a certain type of humor. I have good days and I have bad days. I tell clean jokes and I tell dick jokes, and not everybody's going to agree with that. It wasn't until later on that I realized that the fans wanted to see something in particular and the [people who run the] house wanted to see something in particular. It created a bit of a conflict."

Part of the conflict occurred on Ian's Facebook page. In April 2010, a few months before he moved into the house, the actor set up a "Randy Parker" Facebook profile so he could interact with his fans. The page quickly generated attention and earned him lots of digital followers. However, there were a few times when fans took to his page to complain about Ian not being at the house during a tour or about the actor being too rushed to give the personal attention the fan desired. While Ian Petrella was at the house, most fans wanted to see a grown-up version of Randy Parker, the affable tyke from their favorite holiday film.

In addition to his Facebook page, Ian agreed to blog for the *Christmas Story* House website during his stay. Because all of the posts would have to be approved by Brian Jones, the actor made sure to keep his comments more polite than he might have been in person. Simply stated, you'd be hard-pressed to find any dick jokes on the blog.

Much to the actor's surprise, even some of the more tame jokes in his stand-up routine occasionally offended a visitor. One of Ian's favorite stories to tell was about how MGM almost didn't release the Christmas film because they were pouring their resources at the time into the Barbra Streisand movie

Yentl, which was released on the same day as *A Christmas Story* in theaters.

"The punchline to that story was, 'Yes, Barbra Streisand was almost responsible for this movie not making it,'" he says. "The second punchline was, 'Just when you thought you had found something Barbra Streisand had no influence over.' Most people would laugh because if you're a fan of *A Christmas Story*, you're probably more conservative and don't like her, but sometimes you'd have people turn around and walk out the door! People would seriously get offended."

Two months later, when his stay at the house was coming to an end, Ian and Brian Jones discussed the option of him returning during the holiday season. For both parties, this was an easy decision. Instead of packing up and leaving, Ian stayed at the house through September and October, and in the following month, he went back to meeting and greeting fans.

He didn't anticipate there being any difference between the two sessions, but there was. Nearly a thousand people a day walked through the front door of the *Christmas Story* House during the winter months, which kept Ian incredibly busy. The length of the tours was shortened, the crowds

© Meredith Poczkalski

were larger, and as a result, the Ian Petrella Q&A was scrapped. Instead, after the tour, the actor would shake hands and meet each of the tourists, offering to sign autographs and take pictures before they made their exit.

The "Randy Comes Home" session was truly a unique experience. It's hard to think of any other place in the world where fans can visit a filming location for a film and meet one of the actors who will give a tour and, oh, by the way, is also living there. The idea was inspired and innovative, which is likely what made it a success, just like Brian Jones' initial thought to purchase the house and convert it into a tourist attraction.

For Ian, the stay at the house provided him with an opportunity to not only meet the fans of the film but also help give back to them in some way. As a general rule of thumb, he never charged EMTs, firefighters, police officers, or enlisted servicemen for autographs or pictures, a courtesy that was always well-respected by those groups.

"We'd get a lot of moms coming in and they'd have me sign a picture to their son or daughter and they'd tell me they were sending it to Iraq because their kid loved the movie," he says. "And I'd tell them to just take it. To see the look in their eyes — they'd almost tear up because they were so grateful for something like that. It was awesome that I was able to do that for them. It was such a small thing that I could do for someone risking their life overseas for our country, but if an 8x10 picture is going to make their day, then how cool is that to be the person to help cheer them up?"

That isn't to say that living at the *Christmas Story* House didn't have its drawbacks. For one, Ian still had to do all of the domestic chores that came with being a tenant, like raking leaves or shoveling snow. Occasionally, people would drive by and recognize him, which usually prompted the actor to tell them that he was just the person in charge of the buildings and grounds.

Another situation that yielded odd outcomes was whenever Ian would have food delivered to the house. After the address was given, he usually had a difficult time convincing the restaurant that he wasn't a prank caller.

"Is it a house or an apartment," the person at the restaurant would ask.

"Oh, it's a house all right."

"Whaddaya mean?"

"It's the *Christmas Story* House." There'd be silence.

"Look, we ain't delivering a pizza to the *Christmas Story* House. If you're callin' to waste our . . ."

"No, trust me. I'm at the *Christmas Story* House. Give me a call when you're outside and I'll meet you."

And when the delivery person arrived, there would be disbelief on his face as Ian emerged from inside the house in pajamas, a light jacket, and with a fistful of money.

Visitors to the house would sometimes also add an unwanted dash of spontaneity to Ian's day. During one Q&A session, a woman forcibly pushed him to the point where he stumbled and nearly fell down.

"What the hell did you do that for?" Ian was undeniably ticked off.

"I wanted to push you on the ground and see if you'd have trouble getting up."

As Ian considered the absurdity of what had just happened, his anger mounted. He ended the encounter with a statement that was part-joke, part-warning: "You [are] lucky I'm not Christian Bale or Sean Penn. I guarantee you that if I were one of them, you'd be knocked out on the floor."

When the December season wrapped, Ian thought that his tenure at the house was likely over for good. He had enjoyed his experience, but he felt the idea had grown old. "If I were to go back, I would only maybe keep it to a weekend," he says. "When you do things with this film, you only get one or two bites at the apple. The first season everyone was really excited.

The Pocakalski family poses with Ian Petrella
© Meredith Poczkalski

Fans Michael Miller and Kyle Mueller with Ian Petrella
© Michael Miller

A CHRISTMAS STORY

The second season, everyone was even more excited because I was back. After that, you're done, or it turns into, 'Wow, how sad. He's still there? Poor guy.'"

Despite his thoughts, fans may feel to the contrary. To this day, Ian still receives emails and Facebook messages asking him if he's still at the house or when he'll be coming back. If those questions grow into a real grassroots movement to see him return, the actor says he would consider trying to work that out with Brian Jones once again — but he's not holding his breath for that to happen.

"You have to cut it eventually," he says with a sigh. "On to the next thing."

CHAPTER EIGHT

Zack *the Bully,* Toady, *and* Nameless Victim

"Zack? It's me, Scotty!"

It was October 2006 and Zack Ward, the actor who played Scut Farkus, was at his home in Valley Village, California. He had gotten used to the occasional phone call from Scott Schwartz, the actor who'd played Flick, sometimes to ask him to participate in a *Christmas Story*-related event, sometimes just to shoot the shit, but this call sounded different. There was urgency in Schwartz's voice.

"Hey, what's up, buddy?"

"Well, Joel wants to talk to you! I have some good news for you, man — you're gonna be an action figure!"

For Ward, this was certainly good, but confusing, news. Over the preceding four years, a significant amount of *Christmas Story* merchandise had been released, but with one notable limitation. "All this product was coming out and I noticed my face wasn't on any of it," Ward explains. "It sort of hurt my feelings a little bit. There were lunchboxes and popcorn containers and all this cool stuff. I'm a comic book nerd and what young man worth his salt doesn't want an action figure made of him? You'd have to be inhuman to not want an action figure. So I had seen all the action figures of everyone else and I never knew why I didn't have one."

His curiosity led him to call a friend who worked in the marketing department at Warner Bros. The friend volunteered to do some poking around to try to figure out why Scut Farkus had been withheld from appearing on any *Christmas Story* merchandise.

"Dude, they don't have your merchandising rights," she said when she called back.

"What do you mean?"

"They don't have your rights. They have everybody else's, but they don't have merchandising rights for you. They're not allowed to make anything with your face on it."

"That's strange. I wonder why that is."

In the months that followed, Ward found out exactly why that was. He describes the reason as only he could, as "a fuck-up in the contract." Christmas Tree Films, the production studio behind the film, did not negotiate for the rights to Ward's likeness in merchandising due to a last-minute decision made after the actor was cast and before filming began.

Karen Hazzard, the casting director in charge of finding the actors for the Canadian shoot, recalls the process of finding Ward. "Somewhere it said that 300 kids tried out for that role," she explains. "That's not the least bit true unless they put out an advertisement before they even really started casting."

Hazzard auditioned actors in a group for the part of the bully. The actors would read their lines, be sent out of the room, another group would be called in, and the cycle would continue until a decision was made.

As soon as he entered the room, Ward made a striking impression. "For one thing, I thought his red hair made him stand out," she explains. "I mean, you're going to notice that. Also, quite frankly, although he was a very sweet little boy, he had a kind of pointy face. It wasn't a cute face. You'd believe this kid being a bully."

"I was told I got the part of Scut Farkus," Ward says. While fans of the film easily identify that character as being the schoolyard bully, Farkus was actually the bully's toady in the original shooting script. Instead, Grover Dill was the bully, as he is in all of Jean Shepherd's original short stories.

"I showed up on set and went to the wardrobe mistress and she put me in the Scut Farkus gear," Ward continues. "I walked out with Yano Anaya, who plays Grover Dill, and we went to meet up with Bob Clark. It was my first time ever meeting him. The wardrobe mistress held her hands over Yano and I [sic] and said, 'This is your Scut Farkus, this is your Grover Dill.' He looked up and realized the height disparity. I was about a foot taller than Yano and

© MGM/UA Entertainment / Photofest

© Yano Anaya

this was the first time Bob really recognized this. He looked at us and said, 'Oh, okay. You get his lines, he gets yours.'"

Even though he had endured three callbacks to land his first big-screen gig, Yano Anaya, who didn't have any professional acting credits prior to being cast in the film, understood the reason for the role-switch. "It was more appropriate for Zack to be the main bully," Anaya says. "He was bigger and had a meaner face."

Thus, although no one knew it at the time, the infamous fuck-up regarding Ward's merchandising rights was born. "I didn't know that was anything out of the ordinary at all," Ward continues. "I mean, that *is* pretty bizarre. People just don't do that. It wasn't as if my contract got changed or I got any more money or anything like that. I didn't really think about it as a part upgrade. I had horrendous agents who didn't know what the fuck they were doing, so there was no renegotiation. We just high-fived each other and said, 'Yay!' Apparently, my contract wasn't adjusted to reflect my change in position in the film."

While the other principal actors had contracts that allowed Christmas Tree Films, and by extension MGM, the rights to use their likenesses on merchandise for the film, Ward's contract was written as if he were a minor character. Because the production company had no intentions of ever creating merchandise of the toady, the actor's merchandising rights were never requested or given. Since it was nearly twenty years before the first piece of merchandise from the film was produced, this was not an issue, but once the film became a full-fledged hit and manufacturers were busting down Warner Bros.' door to create officially licensed *Christmas Story* items, it was quickly discovered that Ward was off limits.

However, even with this mutual understanding of the merchandising limitations, Ward found it necessary to deploy his lawyer when he realized that he should be careful what he wished for. In 2006, a company named Enesco, whose Department 56 subsidiary specializes in holiday-themed collectibles, released an officially licensed "Scut Farkus and his Toadies" figurine; they added more baddies to supplement the Grover Dill character. According to court documents, Warner Bros. was aware that they did not have the rights to Ward's likeness and that was communicated to Enesco. However, Enesco proceeded to make a Farkus figurine and Warner Bros. signed off on the prototype.

When Ward discovered this in November 2010, he was outraged. "*I wanted to be an action figure,*" he thought, "*but how dare they violate the terms of our agreement and not get my permission first!*"

The actor's lawyer, Randall S. Newman, whom Ward had already hired to litigate a separate *Christmas Story*–related case, sent a letter off to Warner Bros. expressing his displeasure with the figurine. The two were somewhat taken aback by the company's response: "If you have seen the item in question, you will note that it does not bear the likeness of Mr. Ward," the email said. "Although the hat, sweater, jacket and boots are similar to those worn by Mr. Ward in the Picture, the face of the character is not Mr. Ward's face."

Ward disagreed. In August 2011, he sued Warner Bros. and Enesco for monetary damages due to the sale and distribution of the figurine. For their part, the defendants maintained that the figurine had a "generic face," and that they weren't in violation of the agreement. The case gained national attention and garnered the actor the empathy of his *Christmas Story* colleagues.

"We've had our issues with Warner Bros. and things that have gone on behind the scenes," Scott Schwartz says. "It's very shameful that big companies make big money and they can't seem to share enough with the people that made them the big money."

According to Schwartz, the struggle that has taken place over the last few years between the actors and Warner Bros. has little to do with the fact that most of them were young actors when the film was made.

"We actually have in our contract that we get five percent of wholesale on merchandising and two-point-five percent if there is more than one other cast member involved," he explains. "We actually have those things in our contract. It's not because we were kids that were taken advantage of. That's not it."

So then, what *is* it?

"They have creative bookkeeping and creative bookkeeping lets them get away with tons of things, until somebody actually calls them on it," alleges Schwartz, who was not speaking specifically about Warner Bros., but about production companies in general. "To do a forensic accounting [of their profits] costs between $75,000 and $100,000 dollars. The movie studios know not everybody has that money to . . . get what's rightfully theirs, anyways."

Schwartz, who has participated in dozens of fan conventions across the United States over the course of his career, acknowledges that this isn't a

problem specific to the *Christmas Story* cast. It's a widespread epidemic that is disseminated from Hollywood bigwigs and that adversely affects actors, who often are at the bottom of the bureaucratic totem pole.

"I've talked to people from *Back to the Future*, people from *Dallas*, and people from *Happy Days*, and at the end of the day, they do the forensic accounting if they can afford it," Schwartz says. "The studio goes, 'Okay, we'll pay you,' but why didn't you pay me to begin with? They want to hold onto the money for as long as they can. Everybody thinks, 'Oh my God! You're on a Monopoly board! You guys have got to be rich from all this stuff,' and, no, it doesn't work that way. You know, we're just regular working guys who, when we get a check for $200 from Warner Bros., we get excited, and that's like once or twice a year."

In fact, even though Warner Bros. didn't retain Ward's merchandising rights, they did attempt to enter into an independent agreement with him to use his likeness on the *Christmas Story* Monopoly game, but their proposed terms of agreement were less than palatable to the actor.

"In early 2006, the people from Monopoly called me and said, 'Hey, we want to put you on a Monopoly game. We got your information from the people at Warner Bros.,'" he recalls. "So, I said, 'That sounds neat. How much does that pay?'

'Well, we'll give you a hundred Monopoly $100 bills with your name on it . . .'

Zack Ward,
Peter Billingsley,
and Yano Anaya
© Yano Anaya

'Yeah?'

'Twelve board games . . .'

'Okay?'

'. . . And eighty bucks.'

'What?'

'And eighty bucks.'

'No. No, I can't do that!'

'What do you mean?'

'No offense, but I do this for a living. I've been in the industry my entire life. It's not like I do something else. This is what I do. I use my likeness and skill set to make a living. If I give it to you for free, why would anyone ever pay for it? That's ridiculous.'

'Oh. You sure?'

'Yeah! For eighty bucks?'

'Okay, how about two hundred?'"

Needless to say, Ward wasn't tempted to jump at their revised offer. The board was released without his character represented on it.

Ian Petrella's occasionally problematic relationship with Warner Bros. impacts the way he helps promote the film during the Christmas season and throughout the remainder of the year. "You do have to ask yourself [if you want to participate in an event] every time an opportunity comes up," he says. "What it all boils down to is the most important thing, the film. If it's going to do something good for the film, then it's worth doing."

As a result, Petrella has collaborated with Warner Bros. on a number of *Christmas Story*–related projects over the past decade, including special features for the twentieth anniversary DVD and, most recently, 2011's *A Christmas Story* Scene contest, for which fans were encouraged to recreate their favorite moment from the film. Petrella and executives from the studio selected someone to win a two-day trip to the *Christmas Story* House and what the website describes as a "VIP Chinese dinner."

Despite Petrella's mixed feelings about helping the studio cash in without him and his other actors getting what they perceive to be their fair share, he seems likely to continue doing just that. "Warner Bros. asked me to do something for the thirtieth anniversary DVD release," he explains. "I had my publicist call them to try and see what kind of money we could negotiate from them and they basically were like, 'We don't pay you for this. We're not going to pay you.' It was one of those things like, okay, I could say, 'No, I don't want to do it,' but how is that going to reflect on the film? For me, right now, the most important part is, as long as it makes the film look good, makes Bob [Clark] look good, makes Jean [Shepherd] look good, then that's the most important part. It does get a little bit difficult and hard sometimes, and there are times when you just want to say, 'I don't want to have anything to do with this,' and just walk away, but what good is that going to do? Nothing."

Zack Ward in 2009
© Albert L. Ortega /
PR Photos

Ultimately, Zack Ward settled his lawsuit with Warner Bros. and Enesco over the figurine. When the topic was brought up in a telephone interview with him and Randall S. Newman, his lawyer, it was clear that no new information would be shared outside of what was reported at the time of the settlement. They said the suit had been "amicably resolved" and left it at that.

However, the suit that resulted from Ward's telephone call from Joel Weinshanker of the National Entertainment Collectibles Association, Inc. (NECA), on October 27, 2006, was not resolved quite as amicably.

Weinshanker told the actor that his company wanted to manufacture and sell a 7" action figure based on the character Ward played in the film, but since Warner Bros. didn't have his merchandising rights, they needed permission from him first. Having never seen himself as an action figure, Ward was interested in working out the terms of a licensing deal, but there were some initial concerns.

"You know, I once got a call from the Monopoly people who wanted to offer me $200 to use my likeness," Ward said before recapping the episode for Weinshanker.

"Yeah, those guys. Such douchebags," Weinshanker offered.

The two worked out a tentative agreement over the phone and, on December 20, Weinshanker sent the actor a contract. Ward gave it a quick once-over, signed it, and sent it back.

He forgot about it until October of the following year. NECA sent over a prototype for Ward's approval, and it didn't take long for the actor to feel his decision to collaborate with the collectible company had paid off. The face on the action figure was far from "generic"; Ward's unmistakable features were etched into the ceramic miniature.

The following year, the Scut Farkus figurine hit the market. Although

Ward was enthusiastic about the toy's release, he soon noticed some red flags. For one, Weinshanker had all but disappeared from Ward's radar. The actor had been promised quarterly reports on the sales of the figurines, but they never arrived. The actor emailed and phoned the NECA offices several times over the course of the following year, but Weinshanker was never available.

As the weeks became months, Ward moved the quarterly reports and his action figure to one of the bottom rungs on his ladder of priorities. He had continued working and wasn't interested in launching a full-scale manhunt for Weinshanker. The toy had all but been forgotten until May 2010, when Ward was packing up his apartment to move. "I was in my office, just packing stuff up, and I came across my contract with NECA," he says. "And I looked at it and said, 'This sucks.' I hadn't even gotten any free action figures. I had to buy them at retail price! It was like that. There were people over at NECA who[m] I spoke to when I called, who were very nice people, who actually sent me their action figures and I signed them and sent them back to them, but no one could get me to Joel. I had no animosity toward the people who designed the figurine, but I was fed-the-fuck-up with Joel because I felt like I had been lied to and it made me mad.

"So, I'm holding this contract over the shredder, and I'm about to drop it in, and I think, *Goddammit! No*," Ward continues. "This is not the way it's supposed to work. I'm a Canadian, and I believe you're supposed to do the right fuckin' thing. So I made some phone calls."

It was suggested to Ward by a friend of his that he call Randall S. Newman. Newman and Ward assumed this to be a standard collection suit for nonpayment, and filed with a court in July 2010 under those pretenses. The next month, NECA responded to the suit and attached a copy of a product profit report, which showed sales of $60,000 of the Scut Farkus Boxed Set, which included the action figure with other characters, and $20,000 in sales of the action figure packaged independently. However, the fact that Ward hadn't received his share of royalties for the $80,000 in sales generated by his action figure soon became secondary to another line item on the report.

The sum of $755,533.67 virtually leaped off the sheet of paper, taking them both by surprise. The six-figure amount was associated with the sales of an officially licensed *Christmas Story* board game that was distributed by NECA, approved by Warner Bros., and that bore Ward's license, yet he was never paid for it and this was the first he was hearing about it.

"After they gave us the product profit report with the board game, I went to the internet to look it up and Zack's face was not on it," Newman says. "So we were completely confused."

The two considered the board game's inclusion on the report to be an error, until Ward went to Cleveland that following November for an event at the *Christmas Story* House.

"One of the people I was working with told me I *was* on the board game," Ward explains. "I said, 'No, I'm not. We looked it up,' and they said, 'I have one over here. You're on it! The version you're saying you're not on is a brand-new version that just came out. There was an old version that you were on.'"

As if on cue, minutes later, a young fan of the film approached Ward to express his disappointment that "the game sucked so much." Ward apologized, but believed that the child's opinion was probably an anomaly. *"It's a board game,"* he thought. *"How sucky can a board game possibly be?"* But as of the time the lawsuit was entered against NECA, twenty-five out of the thirty-six customer reviews of the board game on Amazon.com rated the game one out of five stars. An additional eight people gave the game two stars. The reviews read almost as if the disgruntled customers were in a competition to come up with the most damning review. If such a contest existed, these would certainly be among the finalists:

"This has to be the worst board game ever produced," one reviewer wrote. "If I could give it zero stars, I would."

"The designer must have been a mental patient," wrote another. "Whomever [sic] controls the rights to *A Christmas Story* should be genuinely peeved at this blight on their brand name and should never have allowed this unplayable mess to hit the stores."

"After slogging through the first two pages of incomprehensible directions, I actually thought the game was a joke, like an April Fool's Day prank," another reviewer ranted. "It was not. Luckily, we purchased the game for $1 at a garage sale. We overpaid."

Newman and Ward went into investigative mode. They found and purchased the 2006 and 2008 versions of the game, on which the actor appeared. Of course, this posed a significant legal problem because not only had Ward not been informed about the game, but he was also not given a chance to approve the use of his likeness. The reality of the situation was becoming crystal clear.

"That meant that when Joel called through Scott Schwartz to contact me about the Scut Farkus action figure, not only had he built and made the board game," Ward says, "but he had already shipped and sold thousands of units, which means that when Joel talked to me on the phone he lied. He completely fucking lied."

This conclusion was infuriating, but also confusing. If Warner Bros. had been so cautious about not using the actor's likeness on any merchandise over the last several years, then why did they allow NECA to use Ward's photograph on the board game? Once again, Ward and Newman sprang into action to try and figure out what went awry on the way to the toy store.

"It turned out that Joel shipped the board game in August 2006," Newman explains. "The evidence shows that Warner Bros. didn't even see the prototype until October of that year." The estimated number of board games that were shipped before the film company even saw a prototype totals 10,000 units, a staggering number. Warner Bros. didn't know that any copies had actually been sold when they received the sample, but an error jumped out at the suits in the office immediately upon the game's arrival.

"Sample needs revisions," the email back to Weinshanker stated. "Please omit the Scut Farcus [sic] pieces (or provide proof that you have secured the rights to use his likeness). We are not allowed to licensee [sic] [Zack Ward's] likeness."

Of course, this was impossible because thousands of copies had already been sold. Luckily for Weinshanker, he was able to get in contact with Ward and have him sign off on a contract under the pretenses that it extended solely to a Scut Farkus action figure, while in reality, that contract also provided NECA the cover they needed to continue selling the board game.

"He believed that he could fraudulently get me to sign something not knowing jack-dick and he'd never be held accountable for it because who the fuck am I," Ward says. "I am apparently nobody and he can come in and steal my likeness, take my face, take my life's work, and then walk away because he has a very rich company and I'm not a rich guy. That's exactly what he did."

As if enough salt hadn't been rubbed in Ward's wound, after the lawsuit was filed against NECA, the company provided Newman with quarterly reports for sales of the board game that showed that all purchases were within the jurisdiction of their contract with the actor. These also included gross inaccuracies. After consulting with Warner Bros., it became clear that NECA had retroactively fabricated quarterly reports that reflected the same total number of units sold, but not in the same time period.

For example, it was reported to Warner Bros. that over $75,000 was generated in sales from the board game from July 1, 2006, through September 30, 2006, but no sales were reported to Ward for that same time period. Newman and Ward maintain that this was to give the impression that they had not actually begun selling the board game until Ward had signed off on his contract (which he thought was exclusively for the production of the action figure).

At this point, Newman and Ward believed that they had unearthed the last bit of deception from Weinshanker. That is, until they discovered that NECA had also released a 2009 calendar with the actor's picture. Ward alleges that this was, once again, not only in violation of his ability to retain his merchandising rights, but also a direct refusal to comply with a New Jersey judge's order that the company inform the court of all products they released with the actor's face on it. "It was like fraud on top of fraud on top of fraud," Newman says.

Because of a New Jersey Supreme Court case that allows for lawsuits against the concealment of evidence, a separate lawsuit was filed in August

2012 on Ward's behalf against Weinshanker, his lawyers, and NECA for failing to disclose the calendar despite the order.

For their part, the toy company maintained that the actor's lawsuit was filed too long after the incident occurred. Furthermore, NECA lawyers stated in court that the profits Ward claimed the company made were grossly overstated. For these reasons, the defendants requested in October 2012 that the suit be dropped, which was denied by a judge. The two parties had a mediation session a month later.

"The parties reached agreement on terms of settlement," said Kent Raygor, the attorney for NECA and Weinshanker, following the mediation. However, Newman left the sit-down feeling there were still "major issues" to resolve, among them Ward's insistence that the terms of their agreement not remain confidential.

Leading up to his court date, which was scheduled for January 2013, Ward remained hopeful that he would come out victorious. "There's a real villain in this situation," he says. "There's someone who thought he was above the law because they have a lot of money. I don't know how you feel about that, but I'm not okay with that."

"The page on NECA's calendar that uses Zack's image has the following quote," Newman states. "It says, 'In our world, you are either a bully, a toady, or one of the nameless rabble of victims.' It's ironic because Zack went from being the bully [in the movie] to NECA being the bully."

"I just don't want to be a nameless victim," Ward interjects. Even though the NECA suit also includes misappropriating the actor's image, Newman explains that this case is significantly different than *Ward v Warner Bros.* "[In the Warner Bros. case,] it was supposed to be the Scut Farkus character, but there were questions as to whether it looked like Zack or not," he says. "It wasn't like a photograph. It's hard to argue that a photograph doesn't look like you."

However, despite how much Ward was looking forward to his day in court, it never came. On December 22, 2012, just weeks before the actor had the opportunity for the vindication he hoped for, Newman reached a settlement with Kent Raygor, NECA's attorney. The details of the settlement remain confidential, but that didn't stop the company's lawyer from sharing his opinion of the case to ABC News in the days leading up to Christmas.

"During the course of the litigation, NECA admitted it owed Ward some back royalties based on other Scut Farkus uses in an action figure, and had always offered to pay those to Ward," Raygor said. But, according to the attorney, Ward spent months being unwilling to take yes for an answer when it came to accepting the payment the company conceded he deserved.

"This has been a long, exceedingly silly case by a plaintiff who had a bit role as a 13-year-old in a well-known 1983 film," Raygor continued. "Ward sued NECA over a barely visible 3/8" x 3/8" blurred image of part of the Scut Farkus character's face on the back of a 2006 *A Christmas Story* board game. In that image, the Scut Farkus character is hardly recognizable. Any argument that a consumer would have bought that game just because of that tiny image on the back of the box was just wishful thinking."

Ward's past problems regarding his merchandising rights are unusual. Nowadays, movie studios are unlikely to miss or permit a "fuck-up in the contract" that would allow for so many gray areas. Of course, Ward's issues are not only the result of the contractual error; they are also because such a long period of time passed without any *Christmas Story* merchandising. In the twenty years that lapsed between the release of *A Christmas Story* and merchandise being produced, ownership of the film exchanged hands three times and the movie became one of the most popular holiday movies ever. Then the third-party companies descended like seagulls on an abandoned bag of potato chips at the beach.

Of course, it's partially because of the connections that fans make to the merchandise that has enabled the film to grow in popularity. Without the T-shirts, bobbleheads, and full-sized replica leg lamps, would *A Christmas Story* be as popular as it is today? Probably not.

As suggested by Petrella's time at the *Christmas Story* House, in addition to the merchandising, public appearances by the actors of the film are another significant way that the movie remains in the public eye beyond the holiday season. While at these appearances, several members of the film's cast have raised money for charity, been photographed with fans, and sold autographed pictures.

However, as much as the actors enjoy these appearances, they can also serve as harsh reminders that fans are often more interested in merchandise than the actors themselves. "When I was at the museum, I'd sell autographed pictures to people if they wanted one," Petrella recalls. "There was this one guy who looked like he was maybe in his early fifties and he was asking about pictures."

"Can I take a picture?" the guy asked.

"They're not free, sir. They cost $10. Do you want one? I'll sign it for you."

The man pursed his lips, shook his head, and pointed his finger at the actor.

"How dare you? How dare you," he shouted. "How dare you try to take advantage of us? That's just too much; I'm not going to pay for that!"

As the man stormed off, his wife rushed over to the actor to try to make amends. "I just want to let you know that my husband here, he's bought everything that this movie has," she explained. "He's bought all the glasses, the T-shirts, everything!"

The irony wasn't lost on the actor. The same guy who bristled at paying $10 for a signature because he deemed it too expensive would happily spend five times that amount for a *Christmas Story* throw blanket. Petrella took to his public Facebook page to voice his frustrations with the incident.

"Of course, I got in big trouble from everybody by posting that," he says. "For one thing, Brian Jones, who owns the house, called me up and reamed me for that. I tried to tell him it had nothing to do with him; it's just that any time one of us actors wants to do something to make money off this film, people call us assholes. But anybody else who has an idea to do something with this film and make money off it, everybody stands up and fucking applauds them!"

CHAPTER NINE

Applauding the Geniuses *on Cleveland Street*

When *The Hollywood Reporter* broke the news in 2010 that Peter Billingsley, known primarily by his fans as Ralphie Parker, had signed on to executive produce *A Christmas Story, the Musical!*, it was surprising for several reasons. For one, who would have expected that the classic holiday film, which includes virtually no singing, would be the latest in what seemed to be a never-ending trend of movies that were converted to the stage?

Consider the recent history. In the first decade of the millennium, the

Peter Billingsley in 2008
© Albert L. Ortega /
PR Photos

Great White Way saw theatrical musical versions of films like *The Producers*, *The Full Monty*, *Hairspray*, *The Color Purple*, *The Wedding Singer*, and *Shrek*, to name a few. While some of the shows were critical successes — half of the recipients of the Best Musical Tony Award for that decade were for shows based on films — many others were considered cash grabs.

In January 2011, Loren King of the *Boston Globe* summed up the criticism in her preview of *Spider-Man: Turn Off the Dark*. "[*Spider-Man*] is the latest in a long line of big Broadway shows eager for tourist-friendly brand names to sell expensive tickets," she wrote. "Over the last decade, the lights of Broadway have often resembled a film festival marquee."

So, when it was announced that a musical was being made in the image of *A Christmas Story*, the reaction was tepid enthusiasm. The idea had promise, journalists and fans seemed to signal, but the proof of the pudding is in the eating.

Another reason why a *Christmas Story* musical was unforeseen is because a non-musical stage play, written by a Kansas-based playwright, had been quite successfully making the rounds for several years.

Philip Grecian is a man dedicated not only to his family, but also to the theater. In 1999, he had just directed a stage adaptation of Frank Capra's 1947 classic holiday film, *It's a Wonderful Life*, but the script was terrible. As a playwright, he thought he might take a crack at writing a better edition. He contacted his editor at Dramatic Publishing, which licenses shows for theater companies and schools, and asked them for a chance to bring a better version of *Life* to the stage.

It turned out there was already a new version coming out that year, but his editor had another suggestion: "Have you ever heard of this movie, *A Christmas Story*?"

The movie was sixteen years old, and the twenty-four-hour marathons of the film had already started running on TBS, but it was before the movie had really caught on as a pop phenomenon. It was entirely plausible that Grecian's answer would be negative, but instead, he replied with, "Well, gosh, yes!"

His mind filled with memories of the early 1980s. He thought back to when he was a father with young children. He would often read them a bedtime story. Grecian was a fan of Jean Shepherd's work, which led him to share those stories with his children. His kids became close friends with Ralphie, Randy, Flick, and Schwartz, and whenever a new edition of *Playboy* arrived in the mail, they became excited and exclaimed, "Is there a Jean Shepherd story in this one?"

When the winter of 1983 rolled around, Grecian and his wife took their kids to see *A Christmas Story*. They didn't know anything about the movie except that it was by the director of *Porky's* and that it was supposed to be family-friendly. There was an excited buzz in the aisle where his family sat when the lights dimmed, the music started, and the title card appeared on the screen that read "A film by Jean Shepherd."

"*Our* Jean Shepherd?" His daughter could hardly contain her amazement and elation.

As the movie unfolded, it became clear that it *was* their Jean Shepherd after all. They watched, transfixed for the movie's full running time. When it was over, *A Christmas Story* instantly became a Grecian family favorite. The film would go on to be referenced throughout the following years and, when the marathon showings began on television, it became their must-watch event of the holiday season.

It's not surprising, then, that when he was offered the chance to adapt *A Christmas Story* for the stage, the playwright jumped at the chance. Through his editor, a deal was struck with Warner Bros. and Jean Shepherd. Grecian was allowed to use the film as a jumping-off point, as well as the four stories from *In God We Trust, All Others Pay Cash*. The playwright began writing his version of *A Christmas Story*, a process that provided some unique challenges early on.

"When I adapted this for the stage, I didn't have a copy of the screenplay," he says. "I had a VHS copy of the movie and a book with the stories in it, so I began with the stories. Those things that were common to both I circled and underlined, and then I watched the movie and the things I wanted to add in from it, I did."

Those who see the play performed live on stage will find themselves watching a faithful recreation of the movie, although the play isn't an exact transferal of the film's events reproduced on stage. "You don't adapt a film for the stage by just crossing out where it says 'dissolve' or 'cut' and putting a 'lights down,'" says Grecian. "You can't read the play and follow the movie, but my job is to make you think you can. Some of the lines in the movie are in different people's mouths or describe different things. Every once in a while there would be something from my own childhood that would fit, and I'd put that in."

Although there were some structural changes made for the stage version, the character of the narrator remained constant. Shepherd was insistent that his voice-over remain in the play, which posed a central problem. Because theater is a visual medium, one of the cardinal rules of playwriting is that an omniscient narrator can't exist. It's perceived to be boring, at best, and a sign of inferior authoring at worse. After giving it some thought, Grecian settled on an excellent way to include the narrator — for the first time, he would be *seen* in *A Christmas Story*, not just heard.

"Adult Ralphie was written into the play as a character," he explains. "This turned it into more of a memory play. I also chose to have the narrator pop up elsewhere in the story as some of the minor characters that appear throughout, like the guy who delivers the leg lamp and the firefighter that frees Flick from the flagpole. It works quite nicely."

Shep thought the device was a smart way to handle the situation, and luckily audiences and theater company owners agree with him. When the play was published in August 2000, Grecian fully expected that there would be no productions of it that year. His editor had told him that most theater groups had already decided what they would be staging for that upcoming December and that they were hoping it would be a hit the following year.

Much to their amazement, the hit came early. When *A Christmas Story* was added to Dramatic Publishing's website as a new acquisition, close to thirty groups canceled their previously announced holiday titles and signed on to stage *A Christmas Story* instead. According to Grecian, the show is produced nearly a hundred times a year by various groups across the United States, where it is almost always certain to draw a big crowd. "It's pulled several theaters out of bankruptcy," he says. "It usually sells out."

This isn't to say that all the performances are of equal caliber, obviously. Although Grecian doesn't get to see many productions of his show during the holiday season, he concedes that sometimes his plays don't quite come to life on stage in the way he had intended. For him, it's just a side effect of being a playwright with popular material: "My wife and I went to another town with another couple to see a high school's production of my version of

Dracula and it was dreadful," he recalls. "When we got back to my house, the guy in the other couple said, 'Doesn't it bother you to see your play ruined like that?' I walked over to my bookcase, pulled out a copy of the *Dracula* script, and said, 'Here's my play. My play is fine.' A playwright has to learn early on that it's never going to be what you saw in your mind when you were writing it. Sometimes it's not as good, sometimes it's better. Sometimes there are things the director or the set designer does that you never even thought of."

Although hundreds of thousands of people have seen the non-musical adaptation of *A Christmas Story* live, one notable person never had the opportunity to do so. Throughout the writing process, Grecian and Jean Shepherd never communicated directly. The playwright would work on scenes and, once they were completed, his editor would send them to Shep for his feedback. "He didn't want to change anything, which pleased me," the playwright says.

However, with only a few scenes left to complete in the show's second act, Grecian received a sobering phone call from his editor.

"Phil, I have bad news," she started.

"Well, what?"

"Shep died."

There was silence on the line for a few moments.

"Really?" He was silent for another second. "I didn't know he was sick. He never said anything, did he?"

Jean Parker Shepherd passed away on October 16, 1999, at 3:20 a.m. at Lee Memorial Hospital near his home in Sanibel Island, Florida. Grecian was right: he hadn't given any indication that he was sick because, according to his closest friend and business advisor Irwin Zwilling, he wasn't. His death was cited as a result of natural causes. The world lost one of America's greatest storytellers — and the loss was felt by those who were most influenced by his work.

"Jean Shepherd showed me that the little plastic box under my pillow could contain a magical world; that radio could present ideas, stories, characters, and words, in addition to music," radio personality Vin Scelsa said. "Shep taught me that nothing can be more provocative on the radio than the honest-to-goodness sound of an infectious laugh directed at life's absurd and beautiful ironies."

Jean Shepherd in 1972
© Photofest

"Shepherd often said, 'You never know,'" recalls Doug McIntyre, a writer for film and television. "Mostly, he meant this as a warning. But it could also be taken as an aphorism of hope. You never know who you'll influence when you put pen to paper or fingers to keyboard. You never know which ten-year-old insomniac will read or hear or see something you've written. You never know how you might give that young person focus, laughter, a dream.

"His memory will survive his passing," McIntyre continued. "He never achieved 'fame.' He was never photographed leaving a restaurant or walking on the red carpet with a starlet on his arm. He achieved artistic excellence. He achieved something very rare — originality."

Even before the theatrical release of *A Christmas Story*, it was obvious that Shepherd's cultural influence would not be soon forgotten. In 1981, he was the recipient of the second annual Hammond Achievement Award, an honor bestowed upon individuals raised in the Indiana town who went on to achieve national or international recognition. After receiving a letter notifying him of the award, Shep wrote back to acknowledge he would be accepting as only he could.

"Yours is the first letter of any sort that I've ever in all the years received from Hammond, good or bad," he wrote. "I have always had a sneaking suspicion that an undercover Select Committee of watchful Hammond citizens was operating successfully to keep my books, short stories, TV shows, and any mention of my name out of the records of the town, for their own sinister purposes."

But this wouldn't be the last time the alleged "Select Committee" would celebrate their hometown hero. In March 2003, Hammond opened a community center in his name and honor. Five years later, the Indiana Welcome Center, conveniently and coincidentally located in the town, created a lavish display dedicated to *A Christmas Story* that lasted throughout the entire holiday season.

"*A Christmas Story* Comes Home," as the exhibition was called, included six animatronic displays depicting scenes from the movie, which were

Yano Anaya, Ian Petrella, Zack Ward, Scott Schwartz, and Tedde Moore at "*A Christmas Story* Comes Home"
© Yano Anaya

previously on display five years earlier in the Macy's window in New York City. There were also activities for families, such as a "Mommy's Little Piggy" eating contest, a "What I Want for Christmas" theme-writing contest, and screenings of the film.

Nearly four thousand visited the presentation in its first three days, and based on its success in its inaugural year, it has since become an annual staple of the holiday season. In 2004, Yano Anaya, Tedde Moore, Ian Petrella, Scott Schwartz, and Zack Ward all visited the Midwestern town to meet fans, participate in the activities, and sign autographs. In 2012, it was announced that the center was launching a massive fundraising effort to erect a statue of Flick with his tongue stuck to a flagpole in time for the film's thirtieth anniversary the following year.

So perhaps Jean Shepherd never achieved fame in the conventional sense, but that hasn't stopped the people of Hammond from treating him like a rock star.

Johnny Rabe © Carol Rosegg

Shep's wife, Leigh Brown, had died a year before him and, with Shep's kids from a previous marriage estranged, Zwilling became the executor to Shep's estate. Once Grecian's play was completed, the business advisor signed off on it and it was able to move forward to production.

Since its debut, Grecian's version of *A Christmas Story* has become one of the most produced holiday shows across the United States. The show has become so popular that many theater companies hoping to stage the production have to apply months or even years in advance, just to ensure that they will be granted a license to bring the show to the stage. Because there are restrictions on how many theater groups in an area can produce the same show, every year some groups are left out in the winter cold.

"That happens a lot," Grecian says. "Sometimes they write to me and say, 'Can you put in a good word?' All right, I don't know you, but I'll certainly send a little note to the publisher."

In 2006, with Grecian's play in its sixth successful season, playwright Joseph Robinette, whose previous credits included stage adaptations of *Charlotte's Web* and *Stuart Little*, set out to create a new and separate big-budget musical adaptation of *A Christmas Story*. Like Grecian, he wanted to collaborate with Warner Bros. and Dalfie Entertainment, the production company set up by Zwilling to manage Jean Shepherd's business affairs, and was granted unprecedented access to not only Shep's short stories and the plot points exclusive to the film but also the iconic logo for the film with the title written in the familiar bold red typeface.

"I did triage," Robinette told the *New York Times* in 2011 about the writing process. "This must be in it, this should be in it if we have the time, and we might be able to get rid of that." As a result, some of the memorable moments from the film, like Ralphie's obsession with *Little Orphan Annie*, were left by the wayside.

Scott Davenport Richards, a New York City–based actor and composer, wrote the music and lyrics. Richards and Robinette worked together, peppering the script with songs like "Getting Ready for Christmas," "You'll Shoot Your Eye Out," and "I Won (A Major Award)." In 2008, producers Gerald Goehring, Michael F. Mitri, and Michael Jenkins joined the team, along with Eric Rosen, who signed on to direct.

That December, Beau Bridges starred as the narrator, who was now simply and appropriately named "Jean Shepherd" in the show, at a Manhattan-staged reading. The show was well received and, the following November, *A Christmas Story, the Musical!* had its world premiere performance at the Kansas City Repertory Theatre, where Rosen serves as artistic director. The run destroyed box office records at the venue and *A Christmas Story, the Musical!* became the highest grossing show in the company's forty-five-year history. Not only was it commercially viable, but the musical also impressed critics and patrons alike. The limited engagement was extended into the New Year — it was originally scheduled to end right after the holiday — and during this time it was announced that the producers were aiming for a 2010 Broadway debut.

But before the Parker family could make the journey from the Midwest to the Big Apple, there would be significant changes. Richards, who had received accolades for his score, was quietly removed from the creative team shortly after the Kansas City run. The composer had long been displeased

with the musical's reproduction of the Chinese restaurant sequence, a brief scene that appeared at the end of the original film, wherein a group of waiters croon a heavily accented version of "Deck the Halls."

Even though he was unhappy about its addition, the scene remained in the show as the producers raced toward their first public showing. Richards states that although the sequence earned big laughs from audiences, it was always a "source of tension," even before the initial New York read. "I had a very strong feeling that I didn't want an Asian kid taken to a musical and saying to his parents, 'Why are they making fun of us?'" he says.

Ultimately, his criticism and concerns no longer fell on deaf ears. His name was removed from the promotional materials for the show and its accompanying website, and his songs were ripped from the show.

Benj Pasek and Justin Paul, two songwriters who were both just twenty-four years old when they were hired to replace Richards, said they also took offense to the Chinese restaurant scene, but understood why it was in the show.

"The only way we get away with it is that it's from the movie and it feels familiar and it's in a bygone era," Paul said. "I think that's why it's excused a bit. To cut it we would be in hot water with a lot of fans."

However, Paul's reasoning may not hold. After all, Philip Grecian omitted the scene from his version. According to the playwright, audiences and theater companies haven't missed it. "It's a short scene right at the end of the movie," he says. "To have people build a new set for a short scene that's all for one joke didn't seem to make sense to me."

One straw that broke the camel's back occurred during the intermission of one of the Kansas City performances. Richards was sitting in the audience and observed a young adult who appeared to be drunk, hunched over and singing loudly to himself, "Fa-rah-rah-rah-rahhhh, rah-rah-rah-rah!" in anticipation of the scene that had yet to come. For Richards, the sight was unnerving and signaled that some in the audience may have come to the show for the purpose of laughing at those whom they perceived to be different. "There was a side of it that seemed like, to him, there was the anticipation of a kind of racist porn," he says. "It was disturbing."

Benj Pasek
and Justin Paul
© Tyler Schwartz

The scene, which certainly does not hold up to today's standards of political correctness and racial sensitivity, is an outlier when it comes to what makes *A Christmas Story* funny to so many of its fans. When performed live in the musical, the sequence always draws huge laughs, but Richards sees a substantial difference between how the scene plays on screen and in a live performance. "I love the movie," he says, "but there's a difference between seeing it in the context of its time, and seeing it live on stage with a real actor. There's a big distinction."

Richards' concerns do raise a substantial question: How do those of Chinese descent feel about the scene? While one can assume that some must be at least mildly offended by the joke, some believe the scene is all in good fun.

"I never saw anything wrong with it," Valerie Mah, the wife of the late Daniel Mah, says. "I always understood it was a joke. Some people get worked up about that sort of thing, but not me."

Daniel Mah was one of the waiters in the movie, along with headwaiter Dr. John Wong, Johan Sebastian Wong, and Fred Lee. According to his wife, Mah was hired through Faces & Places Talent Agency in Toronto, along

with the other actors. When he was instructed to sing off-key it was an easy request. He came from a musical family but had always been the odd man out for his inability to carry a tune. *A Christmas Story* ended up being a perfect opportunity for the actor, and proof that everyone really does possess a unique talent — even if it is bad singing.

Ironically, as easy as the singing was for all of the actors, it was the talking that provided the biggest challenge. All of the actors were Canadian-born, and a speech therapist was brought in to help them achieve a stereotypical heavy Chinese accent.

Mah kept in touch with the other actors and they would get a kick out of watching *A Christmas Story* with their friends and families during the holiday season. They didn't expect the movie to have the legs it did, and they certainly weren't expecting to continue to receive residual checks after three decades. "I still get royalties," Valerie Mah says. "We joke that [Daniel's] still sending us money even after he passed on. There isn't much after the many deductions, but it's the thought."

For Mah's family, the scene has always been something to be proud of. In fact, when they were told that the Chinese restaurant was omitted from Philip Grecian's production, the reaction was extreme disappointment. "I don't know how Daniel would feel about that," Valerie says. "That was his big moment."

Besides the dust-up over the show's final scene, the other significant change that took place for *A Christmas Story, the Musical!* that year was that Ralphie Parker's alter ego, Peter Billingsley, had signed on as a producer. The news was a welcome addition to the creative team and *A Christmas Story* fans, but curious to some of the film's cast members. While the majority of the actors continue to remain involved in promotional activities, Billingsley has elected to make very few appearances to promote the movie that helped put him on the path to being the brightest star of the film's alumni.

Billingsley continued to work steadily after *A Christmas Story* and, in

1990, he was cast in a CBS Schoolbreak Special film, *The Fourth Man*, with the then unknown actor Vince Vaughn. The two were cast as friends and, after a short while, they became best buddies in real life. Over the two decades that followed, their friendship remained constant while Vaughn's career took a drastic swing upward. His popularity reached a fever pitch when he was cast in the 1996 film *Swingers*, which has since gone on to achieve a cult following of its own. He later went on to star in Gus Van Zant's 1998 remake of Alfred Hitchcock's *Psycho*, and became regarded as one of Hollywood's hottest funnymen with his appearances in *Old School* and *Wedding Crashers*.

In 2005, Vaughn started Wild West Picture Show Productions, the company responsible for helping to bring high-profile movies like *Four Christmases*, *Elf*, and *Couples Retreat* to the big screen. Billingsley joined him as a producer and, as a result, has become a high-profile Hollywood producer in his own right.

"I've sort of taken a journey through a lot of different facets," Billingsley says. "I was in post-production for a while and wrote and directed for TV and did other stuff. I just eventually wanted to move into other things. Acting was great but I'd been doing it since I was two-and-a-half, you know. You crave other challenges and you want to break into new stuff."

Although his interest in acting has waned in recent years, Billingsley does turn up in his films from time to time, including in *The Break-Up*, where he appeared alongside Vaughn and Jennifer Aniston. "I did do a little part," he acknowledges. "Every now and then I come back and do a little acting. I love it. I did a little cameo in *Elf*, which I didn't take credit for, where I was one of the elves in Santa's shop. It's fun to do it that way. I acted for a long time and it's fun to come back. And if I'm doing stuff with friends, I got to play a friend of Vince's in the movie and do a couple of scenes with him, so it was actually really fun."

While having Vince Vaughn for a best friend would have been impressive

Peter Billingsley directing *Couples Retreat* © Universal Studios / Photofest

enough, Billingsley is also good friends with actor/director Jon Favreau. When Favreau signed on to direct Robert Downey Jr. in the mega-budgeted film *Iron Man*, Billingsley joined as a producer. The film went on to gross over $585 million worldwide, helping to not only raise Billingsley's profile but also make him quite wealthy in the process.

"Peter is a different duck," says Scott Schwartz. "He sort of swims in a different pond now, with the producing and directing and making six or seven figures every time he walks out of the house."

According to Schwartz, prior to his involvement with the musical, Billingsley hadn't done any public appearances to promote *A Christmas Story* with the exception of some events associated with the twentieth anniversary in 2003. To celebrate the milestone, the cast and director Bob Clark were invited to a screening in southern California, complete with limousines, paparazzi, and a red carpet.

"The guy who [planned the event] was friends with Bob Clark and Bob told Peter, 'I'm going. You're going,'" Schwartz explains. "They were friends and Peter would never say no to Bob. Ever. We did this Toys-for-Tots drive once. We didn't get paid anything, we didn't charge anything, we went there, we signed autographs, we took pictures at this movie theatre, 1,500 people showed up. It was a really nice thing. They put out a nice luncheon for us, for all of us to sit and schmooze. But that's really the only appearance that Peter's done with us."

Schwartz, who owns a baseball cards and movie collectibles shop, acknowledges that Billingsley has helped stock his store with merchandise over the years. "He's signed some things for me before that I've paid him for," he says. "It's not free because he knows that when we go to places, we sell them. If I sell a photo for twenty-five dollars, I've paid Peter to sign that photo. In the last couple of years, Peter hasn't signed anything. He just doesn't have the time and he certainly doesn't need the money. He couldn't care less. For him to even take fifteen to twenty minutes out of his day at any given time, it's just not worth it for him so it is what it is."

Brian Jones, the owner of the *Christmas Story* House, has faced similar challenges in getting Billingsley to participate in promotional appearances. "I faxed him on a couple of occasions," he says. "I don't exactly know why he hasn't been to the house. He doesn't seem all that interested in coming out, so I don't really push the issue."

Actress Tedde Moore, who played Miss Shields, Ralphie's schoolteacher, has also failed to remain in contact with the actor. "I haven't had any interaction with Peter since the day I said goodbye to him on the set, which I might not even have done," she says with a laugh. "I haven't ever had anything to do with him. I completely understand. He's doing his own thing now, he's very, very busy. He's often not available when things are happening, so I haven't seen him, no."

During the half-decade that followed after Brian Jones invited the cast to the *Christmas Story* House's inaugural event, several members of the cast and crew appeared together at public events. For Yano Anaya, Tedde Moore, Ian Petrella, Scott Schwartz, and Zack Ward, appearing together was a defining experience in their careers. Many fans across the United States had the opportunity to meet and receive autographs from the majority of the memorable characters from the movie, all in one sitting. However, for some, the unusual cohesion in their unit caused an arguably undeserved question to be asked by fans at many appearances — "Where's Ralphie?"

Ian Petrella, who played his younger brother, Randy, doesn't think that Peter Billingsley's absence at public events is because he is trying to avoid being associated with the film that put him on the trajectory to fame and fortune. "I'm very empathetic to people like that," he says, referring to actors who resist the pressure to participate in reunions. "If they don't want to do it, then they don't want to do it. They have their reasons. But you also have to understand there's a difference between any of us and, say, like Eve Plumb [who is best known as Jan Brady and has opted out of public appearances over the last several decades]. *The Brady Bunch* has been around for years and years and years and years and years, where *A Christmas Story* has only really gotten its popularity since 2003. That's not that long ago. Contact me in another fifteen years and see what I have to say then.

"But as far as Peter is concerned, he's also got other things going on in his life that he's doing," he continues. "If I was producing and I was directing, then you know what, I'd probably have a different story, too. There are people out there that want to move on from that one thing that they had and that's fine. I understand that. Everybody's trying to move on from that one thing, but given the situation that you're in — where I'm in — if I can use that one thing to help me move on to the next level in life, then that's what I'm going to do. I'm not going to shy away from it because this may be the only option that I have. I have to take it and run with it. If you get to be part of a popular movie that everybody loves, well, see where you can go with it. See what you can do with it. If that can help you move on to the next level, then so be it."

Nevertheless, Petrella still thinks it would be nice to have Billingsley around from time to time. "There's a part of me that wishes Peter would want to do more, but if he doesn't, I'm not going to force the guy to," he says. "He was the executive producer of *Iron Man*! I mean, c'mon, he's doing fine! He doesn't need to do this shit. I saw him last year at the musical for about ten minutes and talked to him and he's doing great. He's fine. He's involved with the musical, so he doesn't hate *A Christmas Story*. He's just moving on with his life. I know everyone asks, 'Why doesn't Peter do this,' or 'Why doesn't Peter do that?' Maybe he will, I don't know. Why don't you leave the guy alone?"

But then, why *A Christmas Story, the Musical!* as the exception to what seems to be Billingsley's rule? When he signed on as a producer, this was a common question he faced from journalists. Was he really a guy disinterested in being associated with the movie, or had he been given a bad rap over the years? "I didn't really talk about the movie until these last couple of years," he said in 2011. "It was always just this nice nostalgia trailing behind me."

However, it is virtually impossible for Billingsley to avoid being associated with the film. For one, even though he has thinned out and lost his signature round-framed glasses, he still bears a striking resemblance to the boy who nearly shot his eye out on screen thirty years ago. "I get a lot of double-takes, a lot of looks, especially around Christmas," he says. "People stop me on the street, say hi, and move on. It could be the elephant in the room, but I just kind of embrace it. There's such a distance from it at this point. I can appreciate it as a film."

Billingsley's appreciation may have come with time, or just might be the side effect of having young relatives who enjoy watching the twenty-four-hour marathon. "My nieces and nephews in Miami love it, and they'll have it on," he says.

Having not attended many events, Billingsley is perceived as the most estranged actor from the film — which is a little unfair, especially considering Melinda Dillon has never granted an interview about her experience working on the movie — but he has actually done a great deal of promotion for the *Christmas Story* brand over the last decade. He contributed to the commentary track and special features on the twentieth anniversary DVD, as well as spoken highly about the film in interviews while promoting other film projects. However, with his busy schedule and seemingly sporadic forays down memory lane, it did seem somewhat incongruous that he would sign on to a big-budget production that must be demanding of his time. What made the musical worth his time when so many other *Christmas Story*–related ventures, like the extremely popular *Christmas Story* House, haven't been high on his priority list? For Billingsley, the answer is simple: "People have pitched me many things over the years," he says. "In particular, they kept wanting to remake the movie. But I think you only remake bad movies. Why would you want to remake a movie that has endured for more than twenty-five years? But [the musical] felt different — more like an extension of the film."

According to those familiar with how the actor joined the musical's business team, Billingsley was asked to sign on as a producer by those involved with the Jean Shepherd estate primarily because they aren't really involved in show business. They wanted Billingsley, being a recognizable actor from the film and a Hollywood heavyweight, to ensure that the essence of the original film was retained as the size and scope of the production grew through its various iterations. In this way, they were able to promote that Ralphie had come home and lent his endorsement to the musical. The advantage for Billingsley was that he was given part ownership of the show and an opportunity to make sure that the legacy of Bob Clark's and Jean Shepherd's work was properly conveyed on stage.

Even though co-producing a musical was uncharted territory for the man who has almost done it all, it seemed as though Billingsley got a kick out of joining the musical's business team. "It is an eccentric film," he said in 2011. "We broke a lot of rules with the fantasy sequences, the intentional overacting. And yet at the same time, the Christmas morning sequence was very truthful and the film is, at its core, a very real portrait of a working-class family in the years after the Depression: there's a little dysfunction in that family, but a lot of love. It really does slip organically into a musical."

Billingsley also elected to share the love with Clarke Hallum, the twelve-year-old actor from Olympia, Washington, who stepped into Ralphie's winter boots for the musical adaptation. "I told him to follow the interest of the character, because you don't want to be a carbon copy," Billingsley said. "And he's such a talented kid. I was blown away. But mainly I told him to just enjoy it, enjoy life."

With Billingsley on board, the musical pressed on. The next leg in its journey wasn't Broadway, as the producers had originally hoped, but a formal "Commercial Tryout" run at the 5th Avenue Theatre in Seattle. Over the course of the 2010 holiday season, close to 69,000 theatergoers saw the show; its box office haul once again made a lasting impression. *A Christmas Story, the Musical!* became the second-highest grossing show in the history of the venue.

Instead of setting up shop in just one city, the following year the producers opted to change directors — Eric Rosen was replaced by John Rando, who won a Tony Award for his direction of *Urinetown* — and launch an ambitious national tour. After spending a month rehearsing at the Oriental Theatre in Chicago, the musical played Hershey, Pennsylvania; Detroit, Michigan; Raleigh, North Carolina; Tampa, Florida; and Chicago, Illinois. Once again, the singing Parker family met enthusiastic audiences and even managed to impress some cynical critics.

"The cast is both experienced and stellar," wrote Chris Jones at the *Chicago Tribune*. "There's no reason why *A Christmas Story* should not be on Broadway next season. . ."

"With a cast of thirty, this is a big show playing a giant house, but it avoids feeling overblown," said Steven Oxman in *Variety*. "That's an awfully good quality for a Christmas show to have, and it gives *A Christmas Story, the Musical!* a real shot at becoming a seasonal staple."

In June 2012, it was announced that the musical would finally be arriving on Broadway, a major development for a show inspired by short stories first broadcast on the radio and printed in the pages of an adult magazine. Previews began November 5, and the gala opening night performance was on the 19th.

Dan Lauria © Carol Rosegg

With the larger-scale production came other changes. Billingsley and the other producers remained on board but were now joined by over half a dozen new financial contributors. The large cast was completely upended: in the initial Broadway press release, no actors were announced as being associated with the show. Auditions for the roles of Randy, Flick, Schwartz, Scut Farkus, Grover Dill, and Mary Beth and Esther Jane, two characters exclusive to the musical, were set for June 16 at Pearl Studios on Eighth Avenue in Manhattan.

One of the first significant pieces of casting news was not about one of the child actors but, rather, about the narrator. Dan Lauria, known to most people as the father on the hit television show *The Wonder Years*, was cast as the Jean Shepherd character. For hardcore fans of the film and Shep's career, the bulletin was a welcomed, if not slightly ironic, announcement.

When the film version of *A Christmas Story* was in development back in the early '80s, Shepherd was insistent that there be a voice-over narration. Not only would it connect the movie with his radio show, but it would also enable Shep to comment on the difference between the 1940s, when young

John Bolton © Carol Rosegg

Ralphie was growing up, and the 1980s, when the film was released. Unlike the other characters, the adult Ralphie could have the hindsight to comment on "the good old days."

But as with most successful ideas in show business, when the film started gaining in popularity, a flood of television shows and films started including narration. When *The Wonder Years* was being developed in 1988, Jean Shepherd was the first person considered for the voice of the adult Kevin Arnold, who functioned as a narrator in the same way as adult Ralphie did in *A Christmas Story*.

"*The Wonder Years* is a bitter story," *A Christmas Story* director Bob Clark recalled. "They first auditioned Shepherd to do that. I introduced him to Spielberg. Steven was a big fan of *A Christmas Story* and he wanted to meet Shepherd. So he had lunch with him and his wife and he called me and said, 'Bob, how'd you get along with this guy?' I said, 'I know exactly what you're talking about, Steven. Jean and I were together on this venture for ten years, so we had a rapport. He's evasive, but not nasty.'"

Shep wasn't cast. However, Peter Billingsley did appear in two episodes of the show, so there was a *Christmas Story* connection made despite Shepherd's absence.

For the musical, John Bolton was hired to reprise his role from the national tour as the Old Man. The New York–based actor received rave reviews in every city the tour had travelled to and, especially considering his proximity to the Great White Way, it would have been an outrageous snub to not cast him.

In the months before Bolton was cast, Scott Schwartz had been keeping his fingers crossed that Bolton would return to the stage to battle the furnace and take on the Bumpus hounds for another season. "He is unbelievable," he says. "He is Jerry Lewis and Dick Van Dyke circa 1965. He is absolutely amazing. That is a Tony-winning performance. I hope that they keep him and that he stays with the show because he loves it. We understand he's not a big name, he's not a big star. He's not Hugh Jackman. I'm just hoping they don't go Hollywood and try to make the Old Man a big star because that would be an absolute shame and a crime to this man because he is awesome. He really is."

Tedde Moore agreed: "I adored the actor who was playing the father at the time I saw the show," she says. "I remember that. I thought he was just terrific."

Part of what made Bolton's performance stand out in the national tour was a show-stopping big production number set to the tune of "A Major Award," the Pasek and Paul tune that may have been inspired by original composer Scott Davenport Richards' song of nearly the same name. The jaunty sequence appears when the Old Man wins the infamous leg lamp statue for winning a crossword puzzle contest. The following five minutes consists of an elaborate fantasy sequence, in which the Old Man and his family become part of a leg lamp kickline.

In developing the barn-burning dance routine, Warren Carlyle, the show's choreographer, said he had just one simple objective in giving movement to this classic story: "Everybody in America knows this story and the

The leg lamp fantasy sequence © Carol Rosegg

© Carol Rosegg

most important thing is not to screw things up," he said. "My choreography looks like crazy Midwestern people opened the doors of their houses and started to dance."

If that's what Carlyle was going for, then he hit the nail on the head. *A Christmas Story, the Musical!* is a great translation because the producers have remained true to not only the original film but also Shepherd's intention for his characters. The first major test was whether or not the story's holiday landscape would be downplayed for the sake of increasing the accessibility of the show, a suggestion the creative team ultimately rebuked.

"There was talking about making this un-Christmas[y] in some way," Carlyle says. "Producers like to make a return on their investment. They'll say, 'Can't we set it in March?' But it's got the word 'Christmas' in the title, so we decided we should embrace that and try and find the magic of what we all thought Christmas could be when we were kids."

By September, a large billboard was erected above the marquee at the Lunt-Fontanne Theatre, where the musical was set to make its Broadway debut. The image was of a glowing leg lamp, which was prominently displayed in the center of the artwork against a forest green background, with the large, red logo for the play over it. On the right side of the lamp was a young boy

The Lunt-Fontanne Theatre © Josef Pinlac

Joe West
© Carol Rosegg

in glasses, whom many probably assumed would be the actor playing Ralphie. He wasn't, and as of that moment, nobody knew who would be starring in the show as the kid who wants a Red Ryder BB gun more than anything else in the world.

A nationwide search was conducted for a new young actor to fill in for Clark Hallum, who had played Ralphie throughout the show's five-city tour. In early October, with only a few weeks to go before the first preview performance, it was announced that Johnny Rabe, whose previous stage credit was as one of the students in Miss Shields' class during the tour, would be the primary heir to the role, while Joe West would pinch-hit during select performances.

"After months of searching, we are thrilled to have found two exceptionally talented boys to play the role of Ralphie," producer Gerald Goehring said when the casting was announced. "Broadway's newest twelve-year-old triple threat, Johnny Rabe, graduated from the ranks of the kids' ensemble in last year's tour to become our terrific young leading man. Joe West wowed us with his online video audition and now joins our fabulous company. We couldn't be more excited to be the first to share these two young stars with the Broadway community!"

Just when it seemed the musical's path to the theater capital of the world was going smoothly, an obstacle of epic proportions blew onto Manhattan Island. On October 25, a Category 1 hurricane made landfall in Atlantic City, which had widespread effects throughout the northeast. New York City experienced major flooding and power outages. Anticipating Sandy's arrival, Broadway theaters closed on the 24th and their doors remained shut until the 26th, one day longer than the shutdown that had followed 9/11.

Even though *A Christmas Story, the Musical!* hadn't opened yet, the aftermath of Sandy significantly impacted the producers' rehearsal schedule. In order to ensure that the show met audience members' expectations, the first preview performance was moved two days to November 7.

The show had its first sold-out performance on that Wednesday. The New York temperature seemed to cooperate in transforming the lavish

Broadway playhouse into the frigid landscape of Midwestern Ohio. From the first note of the overture, the audience remained captivated as they watched their favorite holiday film unfold in front of their eyes, with some small, but significant changes.

Even more than the film, *A Christmas Story, the Musical!* is a story about the big hopes and dreams of simple people. Ralphie's first ballad, "Red Ryder Carbine Action BB Gun," is a driving number with a sense of energy and enthusiasm in which the show's hero imagines all the people he could save from bad guys if his Christmas wish came true. For him, the gift isn't just about childish selfishness, but about being important to his friends, teacher, and the Old Man. In the song, Ralphie imagines his father being so proud of him that he'd exclaim, "That boy, he's my son!" It's a touching moment that elevates the importance of the gift and causes the audience to root for him even more.

"The Genius on Cleveland Street," sung by the Old Man while he's filling out his puzzle, sees him musing about how he could prove to all his naysayers that he is smart and important if he won something, well, major, in a crossword contest. The number adds depth to the character and serves as an explanation as to why he is so excited when the leg lamp enters his life. It also causes the audience to reevaluate his disappointment when it is ultimately broken. For him, it's not about the lamp's provocativeness; it's about his self-esteem and what the glowing trophy means for it.

Johnny Rabe at the Broadway premiere
© Tyler Schwartz

One of the most fun numbers in the show is "When You're a Wimp," which is performed by the schoolchildren, including Ralphie, Schwartz, Flick, and Randy, who is forced to remain with his hands pointed in opposite directions during the song because he "can't put his arms down!" Throughout the sequence, the kids sing their displeasure at being picked on by Scut Farkus and Grover Dill, and fantasize about the days when eating all their vegetables will pay off and they're able to seek vengeance on

their tormentors. When Ralphie beats Farkus into a bloody-nosed pulp in the second act, you're not just watching the emotional outburst of a child; you're seeing one of the protagonist's deepest wishes come true.

Perhaps the most remembered song is "Ralphie to the Rescue," a fantasy sequence in which Ralphie imagines himself battling Black Bart, alligators, and the seven seas to save Miss Shields, who has been kidnapped by a band of pirates. The number is complete with well-choreographed stunts and dozens of dancers. It's easily one of the most enjoyable numbers in the show, mostly for its overly dramatic justification of Ralphie's fetishistic desire for his gun.

The songs for the musical may have impressed many in the audience, but Tedde Moore, who played Miss Shields in the film, thought there was room for improvement in Pasek and Paul's score. "It's not my favorite kind of music," she explains. "It never really goes anywhere. I felt that the material cried out for tuneful songs that kids could sing and they just weren't there."

In fact, one of the most simultaneously lavish and ill-advised musical sequences is an extended number right after Ralphie receives a C+ on his Christmas theme. The scene changes quickly into another one of our hero's fantasies, where this time Miss Shields, played on stage by the talented Caroline O'Connor, appears as a belting 1930s speakeasy performer in a red sequin dress. She, along with the musical's impressive chorus of kids, teases Ralphie about his grade and taunts him with the familiar refrain about his eye getting shot out. The real highlight of that number is nine-year-old Luke

Spring, who has a tap dance in the climax of the number. The moment moves audiences to wild applause, partially because of the youngster's immense talent, but also because a small kid dressed as a gangster is undeniably cute.

The problem with the number isn't the performance (which, in the Broadway production, was terrific), but the song's staging and placement in the show. *A Christmas Story, the Musical!* clocked in at nearly two and a half hours, with most of the movie's memorable scenes frontloaded in the first half. One notable exception is the flagpole sequence, which inexplicably went from being early in the movie to after intermission. However, by the time the speakeasy fantasy appeared, many in the audience appeared to be growing restless from the diversions in the plot. Just as Bob Clark had made the decision to edit out a number of the fantasy sequences from the original cut of the movie, some edits to the musical would have served the story better.

At one point during the performance, a woman seated in the mezzanine section pointed up at the disco ball that appeared on the stage during the tap number and asked the person sitting next to her, "We *are* watching *A Christmas Story*, aren't we?" If the hum of chatter that grew in the audience

Luke Spring and Caroline O'Connor © Carol Rosegg

as the number went on is any indication, it seemed as though others shared the woman's sentiments.

While the musical is a fantastic adaptation, nearly all of the best-loved moments from the film that were reproduced on stage felt slightly anticlimactic. Much of the humor in the movie comes from close-ups and reaction shots — Flick's elastic tongue as he tries to free himself from the frozen pole, the Old Man's look of utter disgust as Randy eats like a "little piggy," and the gleam in Ralphie's eye when he discovers the Red Ryder present on Christmas morning — and it's hard to reproduce those subtle moments on stage. The majority of the laughter in the theater came in anticipation of favorite sequences, like when the mother got Randy's snowsuit or when the Old Man's tire blew, but when the payoff occurred, the sound in the auditorium was noticeably thinner.

Without a doubt, the audience was most tickled when Andrew Cristi reprised his role from the show's national tour as the Chinese waiter during the restaurant scene. It seemed as if the entire audience sang along with the "Fa-rah-rah-rah-rah" chorus, a sight that would surely have made the show's original composer, Scott Davenport Richards, cringe and hang his head in disappointment.

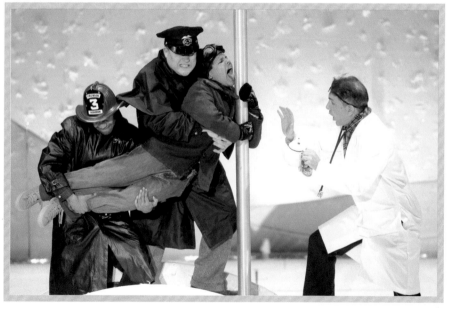

Jonathan Burke, George Wolffe, Nicholas Daniel Gonzalez, and Adam Pelty © Carol Rosegg

Despite some mild critiques, Broadway critics, Tedde Moore, and others in the *Christmas Story* community remained genuinely impressed with the show as a whole. "I thought they did all sorts of interesting, fun things with it," Moore said. "I liked it. I'm a big, big supporter of it. I also thought it was a great subject for a musical. It didn't end up with the sing-songy songs that old-fashioned me would have liked, but tastes change. Everybody else seems to be happy with the direction that musicals are headed in, so off we go!"

"I saw when they opened it up in Kansas City, and it was wonderful," Scott Schwartz says. "I saw it again in Seattle. Overall, it's a wonderful show." For Schwartz, the musical not only exceeded his expectations but also surpassed the quality of one of the most beloved shows running on Broadway against *A Christmas Story*.

"They say *The Lion King* is a wonderful show, but I went to sleep," he says. "It's just very odd, if you're not seven years old. People galloping around in lion masks doesn't really interest me. I went to see it because everyone said, 'Oh my God, it's great!' Now, this is different. It's got a mixture of something for everybody, like the movie."

"I liked it," says Brian Jones. "I thought the stage was fabulous. Jerry [Goehring] really put a lot of work into it. He's got himself a winner there."

"Imaginative, hilarious at spots, heartwarming and just plain good family fun, this new show is a must for the holidays," Joseph Cervelli of *The Record* newspaper in New Jersey said.

"Try enough times to turn a beloved holiday movie into a Broadway franchise (*Elf*, Irving Berlin's *White Christmas*), and eventually one of them has to score," Richard Zoglin of *Time* said. "This is the one."

For those involved with the production since early on in the process, Steven Suskin's review of the Broadway show for *Variety* might be the most rewarding: "This holiday confection has not had an easy road along the development trail; since 2009, it's gone through multiple songwriters, directors, choreographers and cast members," he wrote. "In this case, perseverance — and a willingness by producers to identify problems and make necessary changes — has paid off in a merry way indeed."

Although it may have initially seemed like an incongruous fit to some, *A Christmas Story, the Musical!* found a perfect home on Broadway. When the show ended its limited engagement in January, its future was uncertain, which was fitting, because so was the future of the whole *Christmas* franchise.

CHAPTER TEN

The Shark and the Real Turkey

When the popular television series *Happy Days* kicked off its fifth season in 1977, its producers certainly had no idea they were about to figuratively "jump the shark." In the final installment of its three-part season opener, Henry Winkler's famous Fonz character rides on water skis and is tasked with jumping over a confined shark in the Pacific Ocean. The episode was well received at the time — it attracted 30 million viewers — and the series ended five years later. However, in retrospect, that event was seen as a definitive moment, when

A contestant in a
Christmas Story look-alike
contest at the 2007
convention in Cleveland
© Cindy Jones

the series began to lose steam, forcing writers to come up with increasingly wild and silly plot devices to maintain their viewers' interest and augment their ratings. Less than twenty years later, the term "jump the shark" was coined to describe any series that had lost its spark by resorting to increasingly ridiculous plots, often losing its audience as a result.

Sometimes it is difficult to tell when a pop property jumps the shark, but other times, it's painfully obvious. In the American version of *The Office*, the show began a swift decline when star Steve Carell left the series. Cousin Oliver failed to attract new viewers in *The Brady Bunch*'s fifth season. Has anyone seen all of the direct-to-DVD *American Pie* sequels and, if so, do they admit it? And as cute as Raven-Symoné was on *The Cosby Show*, everyone saw her addition to the cast for what it was — a desperate attempt to re-inject some youth into the show since little Rudy had become a teenager over the course of the show's run.

When producers and executives decide to extend a franchise past its prime, they're doing so either because they think fans can't part with their favorite characters or because the producers themselves don't want their popular properties to stop making them money. Either way, these decisions are often severely misguided. At best, they fail to excite their most loyal supporters; at worse, they threaten to alienate fans and damage the franchise's reputation with the general public.

In 1988, capitalizing on *A Christmas Story*'s increasing popularity, the Disney Channel aired *Ollie Hopnoodle's Haven of Bliss*, a made-for-TV movie written by Jean Shepherd and produced by Fred Barzyk. The two had previously collaborated on several television specials for PBS inspired by the raconteur's short stories. The reunion between Shepherd and Barzyk was a surprise, mostly because it seemed as though the Bob Clark film had signaled a significant turning point in Shep's career.

"I realized that [film] is the medium and I was not going to do any more television," Shepherd said in 1988. "It's too temporary. You work a year or two years, writing a damn script. You want it to have a little life, not just show it one night, and that's it."

But even with his newfound disdain for television writing, Shepherd soon realized that *A Christmas Story*'s success could open the door to more lucrative projects. When PBS asked him to adapt some of his short stories from his 1971 anthology *Wanda Hickey's Night of Golden Memories*, Shepherd entertained the notion, but only after giving them a fair warning: "I don't come cheap." As a result, Disney was brought on board as a co-collaborator. Shepherd and Barzyk agreed to produce the film only after they were assured that they would have complete creative control over the production.

James B. Sikking, who starred in the NBC series *Hill Street Blues*, was cast as the Old Man, while Jerry O'Connell, who appeared in the hit film *Stand By Me*, was cast as Ralphie. Shepherd cast himself in the cameo role of Mr. Scott, the owner of a furniture shop and Ralphie's first employer. The film's plot followed the youngster's first summer job and the family's two-week camping trip.

Ollie Hopnoodle's Haven of Bliss was fairly well received by critics. *Time Magazine* pegged the movie as a "Critic's Choice" pick in 1989, while Jerry Krupnick of the *New Jersey Star-Ledger* called it "hilarious" and "super fun." Daniel Ruth of the *Chicago Sun-Times* wrote that the actors "all turn in sweet, endearing, and at times, identifiably grating performances."

Perhaps fueled by *Hopnoodle*'s critical reception, Shepherd kept hope alive that his stories would once again return to movie theaters. He continued to work on a proper sequel to *A Christmas Story* with Bob Clark, and by early 1994 a movie finally materialized.

Scott Schwartz
© MGM/UA
Entertainment /
Photofest

Scott Schwartz remembers the first and only time he watched *My Summer Story*. It was the holiday season and the former New Jerseyan was headed back east to visit his folks. After the plane reached its altitude and the passengers were instructed to take off their seatbelts, the in-flight movie began.

The MGM lion roared and the sound of Christmas bells chimed over a black background, which eventually faded into an image of the familiar yellow house with green trim on Cleveland Street. Snow fell across the frame as an all-brass rendition of "Deck the Halls" kicked in. The unmistakable voice of Jean Shepherd began narrating.

"Sometimes events in our lives come and go before we realize how important they were," he said. "That Christmas, when my Old Man gave me a 200-shot Red Ryder Range Model Air Rifle with a compass in the stock — whoa boy, I'll never forget that! — it was the beginning of something between me and my father. But eventually I returned to the jungle of kid-dom and the Old Man went back to slugging it out in adult world.

"Then the Ice Age ended," he continued with a laugh. "That's what we call winter in Indiana. Anyway, that summer, everything changed . . ."

For the first few minutes, Schwartz had no idea what he was looking at. It looked like his film, sounded like his film, but he knew without a doubt that he wasn't watching his film. When the picture dissolved and the first title card read "A Bob Clark Film," he realized he was trapped on a flight with no choice but to attempt to sleep or watch *My Summer Story*.

Schwartz isn't only an actor in *A Christmas Story*, he's one of the movie's biggest fans. Like most others, he was underwhelmed when he heard a sequel was being made to what he considered a near-perfect movie. However, with his options limited, he braced himself to do what he thought he would never have to.

"Oh geez, here we go," he said out loud to no one in particular. "I guess I've got to watch it."

Back in 1984, one year after the original film's release, *A Christmas Story* had a limited rerelease in select theaters across the United States. Long before its first cable television broadcast and even before the movie achieved cult status on VHS, it was reported in *Variety* that Clark and Shepherd were planning a sequel to the film.

"There is no question we will do the film," Shepherd said at the time. "The question is with whom."

Peter Billingsley, Melinda Dillon, Darren McGavin, and the rest of the cast were all reported in the article to have signed on to appear in the sequel, but further details were vague at best. It was acknowledged that MGM hadn't given the green light to a *Christmas Story* follow-up, but that seemed to be of little concern to Shepherd. According to him, several other studios expressed interest in producing the film, including 20th Century Fox, where Clark had a multi-movie deal due to the success of *Porky's*. Despite Shepherd's professed enthusiasm, there was little to indicate that the *Christmas Story* sequel plans were anything more than another one of the storyteller's tall tales.

It wasn't until ten years after *A Christmas Story*'s initial theatrical run that MGM began requesting a follow-up film. Because Billingsley and the rest of the child actors were far too old to play their youthful characters, it was decided that none of the child actors would be invited back to participate. It's unclear whether Dillon and McGavin were requested to reprise their roles. Shepherd claimed that their initial contracts with Christmas Tree Films included a sequel clause that would have required that they appear in a follow-up film if they were asked. Despite his claims, that seems unlikely. Director Bob Clark had a fantastic relationship with Dillon and McGavin on set, so an invitation was probably extended for them to return, but they were not in the sequel.

Tedde Moore was the only original cast member to appear in *Summer*. According to the actress, Clark called her up and told her she was the only person who wasn't too old to reprise their role. She jumped at the chance to enter Miss Shields' classroom once again, mostly because of Clark's enthusiasm for the project. "It was his dream to film many of Jean's stories," she says. "He really believed in Jean's storytelling ability. He related to it, and he was extremely excited and happy that he finally convinced somebody to give him a chance to do another movie based on Jean's work."

© MGM/UA Entertainment / Photofest

A CHRISTMAS STORY

Despite Clark's best intentions, complications plagued the production. For one, Peter Billingsley's spot-on portrayal of Ralphie Parker proved difficult to replace. Kieran Culkin, the younger brother of then Hollywood royalty Macaulay, was assigned the tall order of filling Billingsley's shoes.

"Bob had a very, very difficult time finding somebody to play that part," Moore says. "And I found the young lad he settled on to be unsympathetic [in the role]. At the time he was very young and it seemed like he was being pushed into something he wasn't too keen about. He wasn't particularly happy, I don't think, and that showed and the film was doomed as a result." Perhaps making matters worse, Christian Culkin, the youngest in the family, was cast in the film as Ralphie's younger brother, Randy.

Veteran actor Charles Grodin, who had recently become a family movie star after featuring in both *Beethoven* films, was cast as the Old Man, while Mary Steenburgen was cast as the mother. Their performances received mixed reviews not only from fans of the original film but also from *Christmas Story* alumni.

Kieran and Christian Culkin in *My Summer Story*. © Metro-Goldwyn-Mayer (MGM) / Photofest

"I thought it was a good movie," Zack Ward says. "But I think because it was *My Summer Story*, audiences just sort of saw it as a vague and non-specific reference to childhood. It didn't connect with the audience as specifically as *A Christmas Story*. The original film has a classical heroic structure. That's what made it work so well. When they removed all those characters and made a movie that didn't follow that structure, I think the audience felt cheated."

"I like Charles Grodin in pretty much everything that he does," Scott Schwartz says. "And if I hadn't seen *A Christmas Story*, I probably would have liked him in this, but everything he's doing, you're comparing Charles Grodin to Darren McGavin. It doesn't work. Charles Grodin is great, but you can't do Darren McGavin.

"Mary Steenburgen is the opposite of what Melinda Dillon is," he continues. "Melinda Dillon is very sort of shy and sweet and kind and quiet, and Mary Steenburgen is a very outgoing actress. So again, in the comparison, you can't say one is better or worse because it's completely different."

Not everyone who saw the film thought the performances in *My Summer Story* were subservient to the actors in the original film. *Entertainment Weekly* wrote that "the all-new cast members define their characters more sharply: Kieran Culkin makes a savvier Ralph; Mary Steenburgen, a snappier mom; Charles Grodin, a loonier, less fearsome dad (despite his clenched teeth and an almost constipated delivery)."

But by the time *My Summer Story* was released, *A Christmas Story* had become a pop culture force to be reckoned with. With only one returning cast member, and in a cameo appearance at that, the conventional wisdom was that the sequel must not have been that good. The film was viewed by many as a "cash grab," in the words of Scott Schwartz, instead of as a nostalgic return to a series of tales Bob Clark loved.

Still, while the performances are somewhat uneven — and, yes, Charles Grodin does give a somewhat awkward portrayal as the patriarch of the Parker family — the story is interesting enough to keep a watcher engaged and some of the vignettes are downright hilarious. In one of the best scenes, Mrs. Parker starts an all-out attack of housewives hurling porcelain gravy boats at a manipulative movie theater owner. It's a great moment, and the movie has quite a few of them, but they have left as much of an impression on *Christmas Story* fans as the metaphorical falling tree in an empty forest.

During filming, the new cast members remained optimistic that their film would find an audience and share Jean Shepherd's stories with a new generation of moviegoers. For Mary Steenburgen, the shoot was enjoyable, especially on the day when she discovered love had been blossoming in front of her eyes.

"Sandra, our script supervisor, and Stan Cole, our editor, unbeknownst to us had fallen in love during filming and said they wanted to get married," she says. Not only were they planning a quick marriage, but they wanted to do it on the set of the film. Steenburgen was asked to be the matron of honor, a role she intended to play with the same enthusiasm she brought to her portrayal of Ralphie's mother. "It was such a crazy honor," she says.

Despite the distinction, the actress' involvement with the wedding didn't exactly go as planned. In the last couple weeks of filming, Steenburgen had gone through a romantic breakup. She found herself up late at night, not getting much sleep, and having to return to the set the next day overly tired. The wedding was planned at the end of the last day of shooting. "I was really punchy," she says. "It was one of those nights where we kept shooting.

I think there were lots of little shots that we left until the last minute. But nonetheless, we all were there for this little on-the-set impromptu wedding."

To this day, Steenburgen believes love must have been in the air that night. After the wedding, the actress was driven to the airport to fly to San Francisco for a meeting to see if she got along with actor Ted Danson. If so, she would be cast as his leading lady in *Pontiac Moon*. She had been up for nearly two days straight, but when she got to the dinner meeting over 2,000 miles away, she immediately hit it off with Danson. Not only did she star opposite him in the movie, the two also married the following year.

The experience of filming *My Summer Story* wasn't enjoyable for everyone. Even though Tedde Moore filmed as Miss Shields for only a few days, she found the experience to be distinctively unlike her time working on *A Christmas Story*. "It was a different film," she says. "It was different for me because I wasn't pregnant, and my ten-year-old son was on the set with me. In fact, I had to actually ask him to step out of the set while I was doing one part of the scene because I simply couldn't concentrate with him watching me browbeating this other kid. It was different for me. It wasn't quite the artistic experience I've [sic] had the first time. It was more workaday."

"There was definitely a different approach to it, even though it was Bob and Jean," Ian Petrella says. "*My Summer Story* is really more about the family as opposed to *A Christmas Story*, which was more about Ralphie. They were working with different actors, and it did seem like they were taking a different approach as to how it was told and how the actors portrayed the characters, but that's just filmmaking."

While the city of Cleveland had opened its arms wide to the *Christmas Story* film crew in 1983, it didn't take long for the *Summer Story* team to wear out their welcome a decade later. Shepherd, who had an increased role on this film as an executive producer in addition to cowriter and narrator, was a strong advocate of returning to the Midwestern city to film.

"When we filmed *A Christmas Story* here ten years ago, I knew it would be the perfect location for the sequel," he explained in 1994. "As a matter of fact, shooting it here was one of my ironclad rules in dealing with the studio. There's just something about this area — the view of the mills, the trees, the houses and people. It just feels right."

Some of the local Clevelanders didn't return the nostalgic feeling. Local journalists reported on the disruption the filming was causing in the city. The press painted the scene of Hollywood big-shots coming to town, inconveniencing the locals with their loud machinery, bright lights, ramshackle sets, and disregard for their simple way of life.

"I don't know who the hell they think they are, coming in here and taking over like this," snapped Frances Andrus, a then forty-seven-year-old woman who attracted the attention of a local reporter. "I been here since 1947, and nobody asked me nothing about this."

"Ma'am, please ma'am," said a woman with a clipboard, who rushed over to Andrus as filming was about to resume. "Quiet, pleeease."

"Yeah, quiet please, yourself," Andrus muttered under her breath in disgust.

Fan Ray Bigness' leg lamp tattoo © Ray Bigness

When *My Summer Story* wrapped, its future was immediately called into question. The film was made for $15 million, over three times the budget of *A Christmas Story*. With the public's interest in the film virtually nonexistent, MGM decided to give the film a minimal theatrical release. Perhaps anticipating unfair comparisons to its predecessor, before its release in September 1994 MGM made an eleventh-hour decision to change the name from *My Summer Story*, which would have helped identify it as a sequel to *A Christmas Story*, to *It Runs in the Family*. This even confused the actors who appeared in the movie, who believe to this day that the decision to disassociate the sequel with the popular original film helped make what was probably predestined to be a bad situation even worse.

"I actually was not thrilled when I learned the movie [title] was changed," Mary Steenburgen says. "I don't know all the reasons why it was changed, but it felt to me like it wasn't done by the people there making the movie. It just felt to me like it would cause people to not realize that we were continuing that wonderful story."

"[*My Summer Story*] never caught on, and I think it's largely because they chose not to exploit the connection to *A Christmas Story*," says Troy Stevens, an actor in the film.

After just a few weeks and $70,936 earned at the multiplex, the film disappeared from theaters. Perhaps as an acknowledgment of their error, the original title was restored to the movie when it was released on home video. By then, the damage was done and very little has occurred to change the perception that *My Summer Story* is a movie to be avoided at all costs.

Curiously, the *Christmas Story* follow-up seems to have in no way

Bob Clark in 1984
© Photofest

harmed the integrity of the original film. For fans really in the know, it's an odd footnote to the story of the movie's ascent to the pop culture stratosphere; to the everyday population, it's a picture that has long since been forgotten, if it was even known at all.

And perhaps Jean Shepherd preferred it that way. "That one's a real turkey," he once said, in reference to the sequel. Scott Schwartz certainly agrees.

But *My Summer Story* isn't really thought of as the moment when the *Christmas Story* franchise jumped the shark. The movie failed to impress at the box office, is hard to find on DVD, and rarely airs on television. Because the film was produced by MGM, and Warner Bros. owns the rights to the original film, the two companies have been unable — and in the case of Warner, probably unwilling — to publicly connect the two films since its initial release.

The shark jumping allegations didn't really begin until Warner Bros. announced in early 2012 that they were casting *A Christmas Story 2*. The reaction was a loud groan from *Christmas Story* fans around the world, who took to the internet to voice their displeasure.

Ian Petrella was on the frontlines trying to quiet the early rush to judgment about the sequel. He attempted to help the producers find young actors to play Ralphie, Flick, Schwartz, and his own character, Randy, and took to Facebook to ask his fans to send any kids they knew who fit the bill to the casting directors' attention. Many on his page expressed concern that the film would fail to live up to its original, but Petrella urged them to reserve their judgment.

One of the main concerns was that Jean Shepherd and Bob Clark wouldn't be involved. In 2007, Clark and his son Ariel were killed in a tragic car accident in Los Angeles by a drunk driver. The loss was one that resonated deeply with the cast and crew of *A Christmas Story*.

"The whole movie is Bob, really, if you think about it," Petrella says. "It was his dream. It was his Red Ryder. It's Jean's story, but it's Bob's film. Every ounce of that man was put into this film. I never got the chance to ask him [his thoughts on the film] and that's the sad part. There are lots of people from this film that I never got the chance to ask those sorts of questions, and I never will. They were all taken from us."

The sequel moved forward with no one from the original film involved, despite Petrella's best efforts. Daniel Stern, who co-starred in *Home Alone*, was cast as the Old Man. While his recognizable name and face were associated with the film, which no doubt provided the perception of a small life preserver on what appeared to be a ship destined to sink, the rest of the cast was rounded out with virtual unknowns.

When the trailer appeared for *A Christmas Story 2*, which Warner Bros. dubbed as the "official sequel" in an attempt to steal that distinction back from *My Summer Story*, fans collectively lost their minds. Bloggers from all corners of the web took to their keyboards to express not only their displeasure but also their deep-seated hatred for those responsible.

In a post about the film, the website *IWatchStuff* posted the following: "With little regard toward shooting our nostalgia out, Warner has decided that the film they've dubbed 'the most beloved Christmas story of all time' is in need of an instantly less-beloved straight-to-video sequel." Other citizen-journalists were less kind.

Russ Fischer of *SlashFilm* said, "I'm trying to come up with anything substantial to say about that trailer, but for the most part it is just sad."

MSN.com reported, "That the thoughtful classic would be tied to this blatant rip-off is making YouTube commenters see red, and clearly the producers had their eyes only on the green."

Dave Trumbore of *Collider* wrote, "In the true spirit of the holiday, *A Christmas Story 2* seeks to feed off of the nostalgia for the original film like a parasite and trick you into wasting your hard-earned money. Season's greetings!"

Rollin Bishop from *Geek-O-System* stated, "If you've ever wanted to convince someone that there really are vile people out there looking to mine childhood nostalgia for golden nuggets of currency, might we humbly suggest that you point them to this trailer for *A Christmas Story 2*."

Alicia Lutes of *Hollywood.com* said, "Cult-like holiday classic and my mother's all-time favorite film, *A Christmas Story* has a sequel. 'At long last!' screamed nobody. 'You're welcome,' said Hollywood."

Among the actors in the original film, the reactions to the trailer were decisively more mixed.

"I was left with the feeling that it is such a tragedy that Bob did not live long enough to [make this film]," Tedde Moore says. "It probably would have had a story somewhat like the one we now seem to have, but I can see from the few frames that are in the trailer that it does not have the same loving touch. The key is always love. Not 'like' or 'be like' but love, as in caring and understanding. It is very hard to judge from a trailer, but I was just left with the feeling of missing Bob. We'll see how the audience feels! They are the arbiters."

"They seem to have done a good job capturing the style and period of the film," Ian Petrella says. "It seems like they kept with the idea of *Mad Magazine* meets Norman Rockwell, like the first one."

"My initial response to the trailer is that is feels stiff and forced," Zack Ward admits. "Not to be unkind to the actors, but it looks like they're trying to fill other people's shoes and it's not a comfortable fit. The original was politically incorrect in so many ways: kids getting bullied and fighting, 'mocking' the Chinese, saying 'fudge' when we all know he said 'fuck,' the father being a hard ass. You can't do those things in PG-rated films anymore without pissing off some parental group, so the script has to be 'sanitized for our protection' and it takes away all the natural flavors that make it feel real to us. Just my thoughts from the trailer," he added. "I could be wrong."

Some believe that whether or not *A Christmas Story 2* is actually any good is beside the point. In the last decade, fans have been inundated with their favorite film, but has it all become too much? Is the film still growing in popularity, or have the stage adaptations, the endless deluge of merchandise, the unwanted sequels, and that little tourist attraction in the heart of Cleveland helped the movie jump the shark?

"*A Christmas Story* is probably at saturation point," says Tyler Schwartz. "It's not going to get any bigger. In fact, it might be slightly on the decline. These things go in cycles."

"I actually thought that once we had the twentieth anniversary, it was done," Ian Petrella says. "I thought once they started merchandising it, it was done. Once you start shoving it

The scene from one of the *Christmas Story* conventions
© Tyler Schwartz

A CHRISTMAS STORY

down people's throats, it's done. But it sort of seemed like it just gained steam. I don't think that this movie is ever really going to die in everybody's hearts. It's always going to be there. There may be a time when people aren't going to want to go to the house or buy leg lamps, that's probably all going to go away. This isn't a merchandise film, but I think because this is a movie that everyone basically discovered on their own on cable and VHS, it's going to live on in their hearts. And that's what matters. That's what's important."

As Fred Fox Jr., the writer of the shark-jumping episode of *Happy Days* noted in 2010, people still love *Happy Days*, even though it inadvertently inspired a phrase that has become synonymous with the demise of a successful franchise. Likewise, it seems unlikely that anything will take away the sentimentality one feels when Ralphie Parker discovers his Red Ryder BB

© David Monseur

gun on Christmas morning. Parents will still sit down with their children and laugh when Flick gets stuck to the flagpole, and will still consider asking them to eat "like the little piggies" when they become disagreeable at the dinner table. Even if the blogosphere continues to cite *A Christmas Story 2* as the worst sequel in the history of film, and they very well may, it won't diminish the joy millions of people worldwide have for what is considered by many to be the best holiday film of all time.

"There are a gazillion movies that are made every decade, but how many of them stick on the wall?" Scott Schwartz asks. "There's just not many on that list, and fortunately enough, I'm a small part of one that stuck. We're going on thirty years and it's not slowing down; it just keeps going."

Like Rudolph, Ebenezer Scrooge, and the jolly fat man himself, *A Christmas Story* is likely to remain a staple of the holiday season for decades to come. It doesn't take much internet searching to find pictures of men and women dressed up like Ralphie in his bunny suit pajamas or a giant leg lamp for Halloween. The *Christmas Story* House and Museum continue to attract fans from across North America, and its founder Brian Jones has even become a pseudo-celebrity in his own right, having appeared in a special for the *TV Guide Network* about the film and a Best Buy commercial in 2012. *A Christmas Story* consistently averages sales of over 100,000 DVD and Blu-ray copies a week during the holiday season, while even the much disparaged "official sequel" averaged 50,000 copies in its first two weeks of release. *A Christmas Story, the Musical!* grossed over $5 million during its Broadway run, outperforming much anticipated musical revivals of *Annie* and *Elf* throughout the holiday season. As mentioned earlier, the musical also shattered box office records at the Broadway theater where it ran. In the week leading up to Christmas 2012, the show grossed almost $1.5 million, an improvement over the stage adaptation of *The Addams Family*, which earned just over $1.4 million over the last week of December in 2011. One week later — the final one of its run — the musical broke its own record, earning over $1.5 million.

A Christmas Story, the Musical! © Carol Rosegg

A CHRISTMAS STORY

In recent years, *A Christmas Story* has been cited as the best Christmas movie of all time by AOL, IGN, Moviefone, Hollywood.com, and Film-Critic.com, which certainly isn't bad for a film that wasn't a critical darling during its original run in the theaters and failed to make a strong impression at the box office. The Broadway run of the musical was nominated in three categories at the 2013 Tony Awards, including the prestigious Best Musical honor. The annual marathon continues to grow in the ratings with each passing year, with as many as 54.4 million viewers tuning in at any given point between Christmas Eve and the following day.

© MGM/UA
Entertainment /
Photofest

On December 19, 2012, when the movie was inducted into the Library of Congress' National Film Registry, it was called one of the "important cultural, artistic, and historic achievements in filmmaking."

But what has made *A Christmas Story* so culturally important?

"Everybody's pretty much connected [to the film] in the same way," Ian Petrella says. "I probably hear this a lot more from people who are in the Midwest and the East Coast, but people come up to me all the time and say, 'That was my childhood growing up.'"

"It's a humble movie," Scott Schwartz says. "It's a relationship movie. It's a heartwarming movie. It's something that Grandma and Grandpa remember because they were alive in the '30s and '40s. Everybody has got that one specific item they remember as a kid that they wanted to get for Christmas."

In developing the script for the original film, Jean Shepherd certainly recognized that the movie's plot and vignettes would resonate with people young and old alike. He believed it was a reflection of the power of Christmastime more than about the characters. "Something touches Americans, something deep in his bellybutton, around Christmas," he said in 1997. "He can't really explain what it is about Christmas that he enjoys so much, he just knows that when those red and green lights go up around the street, and you see Santa Clauses walking around with their bells, that something happens to you. You enjoy it. Now, you can be cynical all you want, but you still enjoy it."

However, others credit the film's seemingly unending popularity not to its holiday narrative, but rather the brilliance of Bob Clark and Jean Shepherd: "It happens to be over the holidays, but so many of the moments — trying to cook a turkey, trying to deal with school, daring your friends to do something that they shouldn't be doing — it's just all those things and they become such heightened things when you're a kid," Peter Billingsley said. "It's just so relatable."

"The poet Ralph Waldo Emerson said that 'What is genius is true for all men,'" Tedde Moore says. "These events that Brian Jones puts on at the house, the disparate lineup of people who would turn up, to me, was astonishing. There were white trash people there, there were people dripping jewels, there were funky people, there were bikers, there were teachers, of course, tons of teachers. It was just right across the spectrum, and they'd all stand there together in this lineup just to talk to us about the film. And it has no boundaries, this film. It is true for all men."

In the late 1990s, Bob Clark sat in a New Hampshire diner and overheard the lines from his most popular film being delivered by a family of four a few booths over. The owner, noticing Clark's diverted attention, came over to explain the situation.

"They come here every year two days before Christmas and they act out *A Christmas Story*," he said. The director sat there, listening to the mother, father, and their two kids move from scene to scene with the attention to detail of a court stenographer. "They did all the small parts," he recalled. "It was astonishing!"

And at that moment, he knew his film *was* true to all men, and that it would forever be remembered as a classic.

NOTES

In the first chapter, the framing story about Bob Clark's drive to pick up his date was told in Deren Abram's 2009 documentary *Clarkworld* as well as the audio commentary on the *Christmas Story* twentieth anniversary DVD. The bulk of Jean Shepherd's biographical information in this chapter, along with all of his quotes, comes from Eugene B. Bergmann's book *Excelsior, You Fathead! The Art and Enigma of Jean Shepherd* (Applause Theatre & Cinema Books, 2004). Additional information about Shepherd's life comes from Hammond, Indiana's tribute video to him and the film, located on YouTube (www.youtube.com/watch?v=fa2NnxhhzYE). Jerry Seinfeld's quotes come from the January 23, 2012, presentation at the Paley Center in New York entitled, *Remembering Master Storyteller, Jean Shepherd: With Jerry Seinfeld*. The bulk of the biographical information about Clark comes from the *Clarkworld* documentary, the Internet Movie Database (IMDb), or from *The Terror Trap* (www.terrortrap.com). The information about the real Flick and Miss Shields comes from Mark Kiesling in the *Northwest Indiana Times* on December 24, 2006: "Cleveland Stole Our 'Christmas Story.'" The director's quote about *Porky's*, as well as the bulk of the production information about *A Christmas Story*, comes from the film's production notes that were released in 1983. Clark's comments about being a "bonded slave," as well as the financial information regarding his agreement with the studio, is from a *Toronto Star* article from March 6, 1983: "*Porky's* Director 'A Bonded Slave.'" Additional information and quotes were provided by Tedde Moore, Ian Petrella, Scott Schwartz, and Zack Ward.

The second chapter is primarily based on conversations with Patty Johnson and Ian Petrella. The background information about Higbee's is from the *Encyclopedia of Cleveland History* (which can be found at http://ech.cwru.edu/). Additional information about the construction and design of Mount Olympus comes from the film's 1983 production notes. Drew Hocevar's quotes come from the *Times of Northwest Indiana*'s December 28, 2008 article, "Teachers Recall Roles in 'A Christmas Story.'"

Chapter three is primarily based on conversations with Tedde Moore, Scott Schwartz, Tyler Schwartz, and Carl Zittrer. 40's quote is from Dalton Higgins' *Far From Over: The Music and Life of Drake* (ECW Press, 2012). All of the quotes from the children at Victoria Public School, as well as some of the details about the shoot and the movie screening, come from the following articles for the *St. Catharines Standard* written by Brian Collins in 1983: "City School Show Biz Hot Spot" (January 8, 1983), "Green Winter Stops Cameras" (February 2, 1983), "Students Learn Reality of Acting as Classroom Becomes Film Set" (February 2, 1983), "Snow Brings Film Crew Back" (February 7, 1983), "It's Fade-out Time at Local School" (February 8, 1983). Additional information about the St. Catharines screening comes from Kevin McMahon's article, "Students Chance to See Themselves on Screen" from the *St. Catharines Standard* (November 19, 1983). The information about the production of the fake snow comes from the film's production notes. R.D. Robb's and Peter

Billingsley's quotes come from the special features on the *Christmas Story* twentieth anniversary DVD release.

The fourth chapter is primarily based on the author's conversations with Paul Hubbard, Tedde Moore, Ian Petrella, and Tyler Schwartz. Bob Clark's and Peter Billingsley's quotes once again come from the twentieth anniversary DVD audio commentary. The information about the creation of the leg lamp comes from the *Christmas Story* House website (www.achristmastoryhouse.com). Additional information about the leg lamp, as well as Reuben Freed's quote, comes from *Cleveland Magazine*'s August 2009 article, "The Leg Lamp," written by Kathleen Corlett.

The fifth chapter is primarily based on the author's conversations with Yano Anaya, Patty Johnson, Brian Jones, Tedde Moore, Ian Petrella, Scott Schwartz, Tyler Schwartz, and Zack Ward. The box office information comes from Box Office Mojo (www.boxofficemojo.com). Bob Clark's and R.D. Robb's quotes come from the twentieth anniversary DVD. Peter Billingsley's quote comes from an interview with the actor and Will Harris at www.bullz-eye.com. The quote from Lisa Mateas comes from Sean Callahan's article, "Jean Shepherd's Hammond Holiday Tale Finds a Loyal Following," published on December 24, 1997, in the *Chicago Daily Southtown*. The review from *Cinema Canada* is from an article by John Harkness published in their January 1984 issue. Information about the merger between MGM, Ted Turner, and Warner Bros. comes from "Time Warner Closes Deal for Turner" by Jeff Pelline for the *San Francisco Chronicle* on September 23, 1995. Information about the film's television airings comes from television listings in the *Orlando Sentinel* and "'Christmas Story' Still a Hit with Cable Viewers" by Kimberly Nordyke for *Reuters* on December 31, 2007. Yano Anaya's quote about the cast being like brothers comes from an interview with Ron Scalzo for *Trip City* (www.welcometotripcity.com). Additional information about the renovations of the *Christmas Story* House comes from the attraction's website (www.achristmasstoryhouse.com).

Chapter six comes primarily from the author's conversations with Brian Jones and Tyler Schwartz. Those interested in finding out more about Tyler's journey should check out his film *Road Trip for Ralphie*, which is available at www.retrofestive.ca. The information about Ken Goch comes from the *Christmas Story* House website.

The seventh chapter is mostly based on the author's conversations with Brian Jones and Ian Petrella. The biographical information about Petrella comes from IMDb. The story about the house tenant disposing of drugs comes from an article published on December 1, 1995, in the *Cleveland Free Times* by James Renner entitled, "A Cleveland Story."

The eighth chapter comes from conversations with Yano Anaya, Ian Petrella, and Scott Schwartz, but the bulk of it comes from Zack Ward, with the assistance at times from his attorney Randall S. Newman. Yano Anaya's quote comes from the *TV Guide Network* special, "The Cast of *A Christmas Story*: Where Are They Now," which originally aired on November 26, 2012. Some information about the NECA lawsuit, and all the information about the Warner Bros. suit, comes from publicly released court documents. Additional information comes from Eriq Gardner's article in *The Hollywood Reporter*: "'A Christmas Story' Bully Fights for His Image in Court." Kent Raygor's last statement comes from Mark Greenblatt's "Zach [sic] Ward: Bully from *A Christmas Story* Sues, Says He Was Bullied in Real Life," which was published by ABC News on December 22, 2012.

Chapter nine comes from the author's conversations with Philip Grecian, Brian Jones, Valerie Mah, Tedde Moore, Ian Petrella, Scott Davenport Richards, Scott Schwartz, and Zack Ward. The information about the death of Jean Shepherd comes primarily from Eugene Bergmann's biography (*Excelsior, You Fathead! The Art and Enigma of Jean Shepherd* [Applause Theatre & Cinema Books, 2004]) and his obituary as published by the *New York Times*. The Loren King article that is referenced is "Stage Adaptation Gives Films Second Act on Broadway" from the January 2, 2011 edition of the *Boston Globe*. Doug McIntyre's quote comes from "A Christmas Eulogy for Jean Shepherd," written in December of 1999 and available on Flick Lives, a Jean Shepherd tribute website (www.flicklives.com). The Vin Scelsa quote comes from a blog post (www.wfmu.org/LCD/25/shep2.html). The quote from Shepherd's letter accepting the award was posted at www.hammondindiana.com/award.htm but is no longer available. The bulk of the information about the pre-Broadway run of *A Christmas Story, the Musical!* comes from the show's website (www.achristmasstorythemusical.com). The quotes from Peter Billingsley and the musical's creative team come from articles written by Erik Piepenburg ("That Wish for a BB Gun, Set to Song and Dance," *New York Times*, December 5, 2011), Sean Daly ("*A Christmas Story*'s Peter Billingsley Talks Musical, Today's Child Stars and His Beloved Red Ryder BB Gun," *Tampa Bay Times*, December 8, 2011), Chris Jones ("'A Christmas Story' Comes to Chicago," *Chicago Tribune*, December 5, 2011), and Andrew Gans and Adam Hetrick ("Broadway's *A Christmas Story, the Musical!* finds its Ralphie(s)," www.playbill.com, October 2, 2012). The biographical information about Peter Billingsley, Vince Vaughn, and Jon Favreau comes from IMDb and the Wild West Picture Show Productions website (www.wwpsp.com). Bob Clark's quote comes from the twentieth anniversary DVD commentary. Steve Oxman's review appeared in *Variety* on December 18, 2011, in an article entitled, "A Christmas Story: The Musical." The reviews of the Broadway show were written by Joseph Cervelli ("Imaginative 'A Christmas Story' Takes to the Stage," *The Record*, November 29, 2012), Richard Zoglin ("Musical Treats, and Trials, of the Season, www.time.com, November 27, 2012), and Steven Suskin ("A Christmas Story," *Variety*, November 19, 2012).

The last chapter comes primarily out of conversations with Tedde Moore, Ian Petrella, Scott Schwartz, Tyler Schwartz, and Zack Ward. Information about *Ollie Hopnoodle's Haven of Bliss*, and the quotes about the film, come from articles by Jay Sharbutt ("Jean Shepherd's Midwest in 'Haven of Bliss,'" *Los Angeles Times*, August 6, 1988), and Daniel Ruth ("Fine Casting Adds to Fun of Nostalgic Film," *Chicago*

Sun Times, August 5, 1988). The quotes from Mary Steenburgen and Troy Stevens, as well as additional information about *My Summer Story*, come from the *Clarkworld* documentary. More information about *My Summer Story* is from Mark Faris' article, "Charles Grodin Feels at Home in Cleveland," published in the *Akron Beacon Journal* on August 15, 1993. Once again, box office information is from www.boxofficemojo .com. Information about the death of Bob Clark is from the *Clarkworld* documentary and "Director of 'Christmas Story' Dies in Collision," published on April 5, 2007, written by Valerie Reitman and Andrew Blankstein for the *Los Angeles Times*. The information about the marathon ratings comes from an *Examiner* article published by Eric Fortney on December 24, 2009: "'A Christmas Story' Marathon Slated for 13th Year on TBS." The box office information about the musical comes from www.play-bill.com, while the specific information about the Lunt-Fontanne record being broken comes from articles published on *Playbill*'s website by Adam Hetrick on December 26, 2012, and December 31, 2012. Peter Billingsley's last quote comes from an article by Adrienne LaFrance on December 25, 2012, in the *San Jose Mercury News*: "Peter Bill-ingsley Gets Nostalgic About 'A Christmas Story.'" The DVD sales information comes from The Numbers website (www.the-numbers.com), while Jean Shepherd's quote comes once again from the 1997 History Channel documentary, and Bob Clark's quotes and ending anecdote once again come from the DVD commentary track.

ACKNOWLEDGMENTS

A world of gratitude is owed to Jen Hale, my awesome editor at ECW Press, for her support and guidance throughout this process. I'm so glad we have similar pop culture tastes and that we're able to make fun books together! Please give my best to Nikki and tell her I'm appreciative of her support, too.

Of course, I would be remiss if I didn't thank ECW co-publishers David Caron and Jack David for once again entrusting me to write a book for you guys. You have always been there when I've needed you, which seems to be quite often, and I thank you for constantly talking me off the ledge when I'm perched and ready to jump.

Three members of the *Christmas Story* family have gone above and beyond to help me — and this book is better for it. Ian Petrella, thank you so much for your help along the way. It's been an honor getting to know you and work with you for this project.

Brian Jones, you have been a great asset. I'm in awe of what you created out in Cleveland, and I think I speak for *Christmas Story* fans worldwide on that front. Thanks for opening your Rolodex and letting me raid it. You saved me a lot of time hunting people down!

Tyler Schwartz, you swooped in at the eleventh hour with tons of information that kept me busy for many hours! Thanks for sharing your extensive research with me and pointing me to several Canadians in the cast and crew. It's been fun getting to know you.

Eugene B. Bergmann and Wil Wheaton, thank you both for your thoughtful forewords! I am so honored to have you both as a part of this project with me. Tammy Tunyavongs, thank you for your help with transcriptions. To Terecille Basa-Ong, thank you immensely for your help in indexing and for being an extra set of eyes and ears. All of your contributions have made this book better.

To Josh Bellocchio, Johanna Calle, Angela De Gregorio, Vanessa "Curly Fries" Matthews, Chris Ryan, Fiona Sarne, and Wendy Salkin: thank you for being soundboards for ideas, listening to me go on and on about how the writing process was going, and most importantly for your friendship and love. Having you all in my life made the process a little less lonely.

Irwin Zwilling and Lyne Leavy, of the Jean Shepherd and Bob Clark estates, respectively, have been so generous with me in terms of having permission to use the two filmmakers' stories in this book. Thank you for your faith that I would do the legacy of these two great men justice.

As always, I have to extend my heartfelt appreciation for my pals on Facebook (www.facebook.com/caseengaines) — they are truly the best! If you aren't a part of the party happening over there, you need to give my page a "like" and see what we're up to.

Finally, to my family, thank you for your unending support of my many incongruous endeavors. You are my biggest cheerleaders and I can always count on you to lend an ear or to sell a co-worker a book. I hope you have some sales lying in wait now. I love you with all my heart.

Enjoy the marathon, everybody! Be sure to drink your Ovaltine.

INDEX

Caseen Gaines is a pop culture enthusiast. His first book, *Inside Pee-wee's Playhouse: The Untold, Unauthorized, and Unpredictable Story of a Pop Phenomenon*, received the praise and recognition of journalists from *Ain't It Cool News*, *The Advocate*, *The Village Voice*, *In Touch Weekly*, and a host of other publications. It won a silver medal at the 2012 Independent Publisher Book Awards in their popular culture/leisure category. Gaines is a high school English teacher and the cofounder of Hackensack Theatre Company. He lives in New Jersey.